CONTENTS

Preface 7

Introduction 9

PART ONE

Using Archival Materials 13

PART TWO

The Craft of Scrapbooking 25

PART THREE

Scrapbook Making Techniques 39

Tips and Tricks 49

Making Your Scrapbook 69

Making a Collage 85

PART FOUR
THE SCRAPBOOK DESIGNS

MEMORY BOUQUETS 91

A Garden for Mother 92

Through the Years 97

A Special Grandmother 100

Windows on the Past 102

GREAT MILESTONES 105

The Wedding Book 106

Heart of Hearts 109

Beautiful Baby 110

Zachary's Bar Mitzvah 114

Emily's Sweet Sixteen 117

Fifty Loving Years 121

JUST FOR JOY 127

The Soccer Book 128

The Happy Face Book 131

Josh's First Scrapbook 135

The Face-Paint Book 138

The Baseball Book 140

The Rollerblade Book 141

A Housewarming 142

SPECIAL DAYS 145

Christmas Reflections 146

Valentine Gift Books 150

Back to School 152

A Gift for Mother 155

Birds of a Feather Birthday
    Album 160

TRAVEL TREASURES 163

California Dreamin' 164

Somewhere in Ecuador 167

ANIMAL FRIENDS 171

Horse Show 172

Our Best (Barking) Friend 174

Celebrating Feline Charms 177

PART FIVE

Clip-Art 182

Patterns and Templates 200

For the generous loan of their personal and heirloom photographs or for allowing us to document on film the special days of their lives for our scrapbook designs, I thank my friends, family, neighbors, and associates.

For her creative prowess, determination, and extraordinary work, I thank Lina Morielli.

For his photographic expertise and generous contributions to all phases of the creation of this book, I thank Steven Tex.

For helping in so many ways, I thank Pat Upton.

For their dedication to excellence and steadfast help, I thank Ellen Liberles, Rynn Williams, Catherine Chapin, Andy Means, Sharyn Prentiss, and everyone at Workman Publishing.

Clockwise from upper right are: Cynthia Hart, Lina Morielli (and friend), Rynn Williams. Ellen Liberles, and Steven Tex

CYNTHIA HART'S

SCRAPBOOK

WORKSHOP

Moments become memories;
memories that linger are the
secrets of the heart

CYNTHIA HART'S
SCRAPBOOK
WORK  SHOP

BY CYNTHIA HART

❧

Special Projects Editor and Designer Lina Morielli
Text by Rynn Williams
Instructional Text by Ellen Liberles

❧

WORKMAN PUBLISHING, NEW YORK

············◆·············

For my son,
Thomas Ando-Hart, with my thanks
for all the happy moments and memories
he has given me

············◆·············

Copyright ©1998 Cynthia Hart

ISBN 0-7611-1222-7
CIP data is available

The photographic illustrations for this book were created by Cynthia Hart
and recorded on film by Steven Tex

Workman books are available at special discounts when purchased in bulk
for premium and sales promotions as well as for fund-raising or educational use.
Special editions or book excerpts can also be created to specification.
For details, contact the Special Sales director at the address below.

Workman Publishing Company, Inc.
708 Broadway
New York, NY 10003-9555

Manufactured in Italy
First printing
10 9

PREFACE

Recently, when helping my mother move from the house she had lived in for thirty-seven years, I came upon the memory albums she had compiled while I was growing up. She had always kept the four baby books—two for me, two for my sister—on a special shelf in the living room, and they were an integral part of my childhood. In my books she had diligently recorded everything important in my earliest life—from my birth announcement to birthdays and Christmases, special teddy bears and first dance recitals. She also included items that didn't make much sense to me as a child, like the obstetrician's bill and the label from the first package I ever received in my own name. My father took all of the photographs, my mother organized them: Together, their two loving spirits permeate the books.

I remember, as a child, opening the books and picking out what I thought were the prettiest pictures. As the years went by my selections would change, but one thing is certain—the images in those books helped me define my childhood. It's funny, but as I get older, it's hard to know whether I am really remembering my early years or remembering the scrapbook's pictures.

And now, all these years later, while helping sort my mother's things, I discovered another massive volume, about ten inches thick, that I had never seen. This album chronicled the youth of my father, his family, my mother's own history and that of her family, and finally, their lives together.

I asked if I could borrow all three scrapbooks, because I knew I was just about to begin a book about making memory albums. What I discovered between the thick, padded covers was, first and foremost, the immense and painstaking effort that my mother had put into these books. Then I was flooded with the history of my family, a history that would have been lost to me had she not taken the time to compile all these images and documents, which ranged from my mother's high school yearbook (complete with her simple yet touching drawings) to a picture of my father in uniform with his arm around his mother. There was a picture of the new bride, my mother, a glamorous hand-tinted photo of her in a black lace dress, my father as a plump-cheeked baby, an insurance record of the policy that my grandparents bought for my parents, the premium totaling five dollars (quite a sum in those days).

I was so proud of my mother, so appreciative of her organization and care. I saw so many connections between myself and those people from the past. I peered at them, trying to discover the same eyes, the same face, but also trying to gain an understanding of who they were.

None of this story would be told if it weren't for my mother. What a valuable gift she has given to me and my son, and to my sister and her children. Her pride in it shows, her love shows, and so does her delight in her life, her children, and her celebration of what she lived and what she saw.

While my father lived with Alzheimer's disease, I truly learned the meaning of memory. To keep your memories alive, you must document them. Make it a priority. Creating a scrapbook is a joyous, creative experience and a gift to those you love.

If I Could See

If I could see as far ahead
As I can see behind
There's lots of troubles
I could banish from my mind.
I'd know what to do,
When to do, who to do.
If I could see as far ahead
As I can see behind.

One of my greatest joys was happening upon a poem of my father's in a box of materials that never made it into the family album. I never knew it existed.

INTRODUCTION

Everything we do depends on memory. Without it, we would have no history, no reading or writing, no ability to learn by experience. Being able to recall the past—either a recent moment or a distant decade—makes us who we are.

We rely on certain objects to help us reconstruct the past—a past that would certainly blur, if not disappear entirely from our grasp, without them. Photographs help us remember the all-too-quick stages of a child's growth, a treasured landscape, or our own life's milestones. And by compiling these photographs and mementos into scrapbooks (or, more literally, memory books), we are preserving not only the physical remains of the event but the invaluable story that they trigger in our memory.

It's been proven that the more often you recall something, the more sharply it becomes etched in your memory—like a river that continually flows and cuts a deeper, more definite impression in the earth. So, too, by chronicling the things that are most important to us, we are ensuring that our treasured memories will never fade.

In the mid-nineteenth century, the development of photography changed the way ordinary people chronicled their lives. Photography studios, especially those specializing in portraiture, sprang up in large cities and small towns alike, while a veritable army of itinerant photographers roamed the rural areas, producing the innumerable images that still exist of families posed, often grimly, outside their wooden-frame houses.

The daguerreotype, invented in 1839, used a sensitized copper plate, coated with silver. This plate was able to produce a positive (as opposed to a negative) image. The drawback was that images, once produced, could not be duplicated.

The invention of albumen-sensitized paper in 1850 allowed photographers to produce detailed portraits from a collodion, or "wet plate," negative. Albumen prints were often mounted on small cards—these "card photographs" were in vogue from the 1850s to the 1910s.

Tintypes, prevalent from 1856 until the late 1890s, were inexpensive, durable, and quick to produce. Most often measuring less than five inches in size, the grayish-brown metal images were often kept in albums, which began to replace daguerreotype cases.

At the same time, the Victorians were inventing the art of making scrapbooks. Until the mid-nineteenth century, all illustrations were hand-colored, using techniques that dated back to the Renaissance. But the intricate process of chromolithography, or "printing in colors," with its vibrant, jewel-like tones and its

capacity to reproduce images in quantity, led to the beginnings of advertising. It also made colorful, affordable, detailed printed pieces—called "scraps"—available, and people collected them with a passion.

Yet the modern scrapbook—a collection of both photographs and memorabilia—did not evolve in the Victorian era. Nineteenth-century scrapbookers kept "scraps" and advertiser's "trade cards" in specially designated albums, while photographs were compiled separately. With the invention of photography, families could keep accurate physical records of their ancestors and offspring, which would be treasured by future generations. The collecting of scraps, on the other hand, was seen as a pleasant pastime, but one that lacked the historical import of family record keeping. The current scrapbooking "movement" has no real historical precedent, for scrapbooks have never been used in quite this way before. In the fairly recent past, mothers made baby books, or scrapbooks filled with newspaper clippings of a child's progress in school, or later, his or her professional accomplishments, with an occasional photo thrown in for good measure. But by using the scrapbook—a combination of photographs, memorabilia, and decorative design elements—as a family documentary (often in many volumes), or as a way to capture and illustrate a particular moment in a family's day-to-day life, today's scrapbookers have created a new medium of expression.

The history that one chooses to preserve in a scrapbook is as unique as the person who compiles it. It is not only a chronicle of an event, it is also a one-of-a-kind expression of creativity. This doesn't mean that you have to be a Rembrandt to make a memory book of your daughter's high school graduation—far from it. What it does mean is that the choices you make—the photos, the colors, the stickers, the embellishments, the overall arrangement—even in the simplest book, are all a part of your personal sense of design, and they reflect your unique vision.

Maybe it is too late for many of us to preserve the memorabilia of our own childhood between the covers of an album. But we can certainly safeguard the images and capture the experiences of our own children, friends, and parents— and in doing so we can hold fast to the memories of tomorrow.

USING ARCHIVAL MATERIALS

Documenting life's special moments is as important as the memories are precious. And while it may seem simplest to go to the local stationery store and pick up one of those "magnetic" photo albums or maybe a plain scrapbook, some ordinary glue, and a roll of tape, these supplies simply will not do if you're interested in making the kind of memory book that you can pass down, intact, from generation to generation. Beginning with the album itself, you need to choose your materials carefully: All paper products are not created equal.

Until the 1850s most paper was made from cloth—linen or other rags. With the increased demand for paper products in the nineteenth century, manufacturers began making paper from wood, which was cheap and readily available. Unfortunately, this paper turned out to be much less permanent, and in this century, we have witnessed the rapid deterioration of numerous documents, books, and artworks on paper.

In the early 1980s, the Federal government and the paper industry agreed to set industry standards for paper, which must now have a pH level of 7.5 or greater and be free of chemical impurities. But the standards apply only to paper that advertises itself as permanent. Your average sheet of stationery, greeting card, newspaper clipping, or piece of construction paper has a much shorter life span. In other words, that beautiful love note your husband wrote you on the back of a napkin a few weeks after you met won't last forever. It will crack and fade unless you take steps to protect it.

THE ENEMIES: ACID, PVC, LIGNIN

Standard store-bought "magnetic" photo albums are actually quite hazardous to your photographs. The paper, adhesives, and plastic covers contain acidic chemical compounds that can damage the photos: Even the pages themselves will turn yellow or brown. Many "pocket page" albums are made of PVC (polyvinyl chloride), which releases gases that can make your photographs fade in as few as three to five years. These storage systems should be avoided or replaced immediately, before they do more damage.

TESTING ACIDITY

You can determine if a particular memento is acidic by using a pH testing pen, which contains a chemical ink that turns yellow when applied to highly acidic paper, or blue when the paper is neutral. But you should be aware that just because a piece of paper tests blue now, that doesn't mean things can't change with time. Acid from your own fingers, the environment, or surrounding memorabilia can all cause reacidification down the line. It's safest to assume that all paper has some acid content and to make archival precautions part of your routine.

A scale of 0 to 14 is used to gauge the acidity or alkalinity of paper, photographs, adhesives, and inks. Numbers from 0 to 6.9 indicate acidity (the increase in acidity is tenfold with every number), and from 7.1 to 14, alkalinity. Unfortunately, the term "acid-free" doesn't always mean "safe"—paper or other products may be low in acid but so high in alkaline content that they can also do damage. A material that measures between 7 and 8 on the pH scale will be the kindest to your photographs and other memorabilia. The life expectancy of pH-neutral paper has been estimated at two hundred years, while ordinary paper with a high acid content can be expected to last only fifty years.

Test your fabric with a pH pen to determine if it is acid free. If needed, launder it in hot water and recheck. A layer of acid-free glue can also be used as a buffer. Use an acid-free slip sheet between your album pages.

But while many scrapbooks today are labeled "photo safe," meaning that the sheets are made from acid-free paper, the mementos you add, such as a child's drawing, a ticket stub, a love note, a treasured wedding invitation, or a birth announcement, can deteriorate due to their high acid content and also harm any photographs they might touch. Glue, stickers, ink, construction paper—all of these can contain acid. And while you can still use them in your memory books, your pages just won't last as long if you do—unless you take certain precautionary measures.

Buffered papers are pH neutral and contain a reserve of calcium carbonate, an alkaline chemical that neutralizes new acids that form within paper over time, as well as acids that it might be exposed to from other sources. For instance, when you mount a birth announcement on a buffered page, not only will the page itself remain neutral, but the alkaline chemical in the paper will act like a sponge, soaking up the acids in the announcement. Interleaving pages with buffered tissue paper will not only prevent acid migration but will also help counteract the formation of more acids in the future.

Placing your photographs or scrapbook pages in plastic sleeves that are chemically stable (Mylar is the best), along with a piece of acid-free, buffered paper, will help guard them against dirt, acidic fingertips, and general rough handling. Documents kept in a sleeve will be protected and won't leech their acids onto your photographs or other documents. A piece of buffered paper inside the sleeve can also help keep colors bright. Pastel, charcoal, and graphic artworks should never be enclosed in polyester—the plastic's static charge can loosen the pigment. And never laminate a document.

If you want to slow down the inevitable process of deterioration even more, you can *de-acidify* an image with a process that is used by professional conservators. Treating paper with a special solution (Wei T'o or Bookkeeper, applied by aerosol can or brush) maintains the chemical stability of a document for one hun-

dred to two hundred years. Of course, documents that have already become yellow and brittle can never be restored to their original condition.

Photocopying documents or old photographs onto acid-free paper and mounting the copies in your memory book is another means of preservation. While the inks used in black-and-white photocopies are not necessarily of archival quality, some are acid-free. You can use pH testing pens to test any copies you have made and if necessary de-acidify them, as described above.

Finally, acid and PVC aren't the only

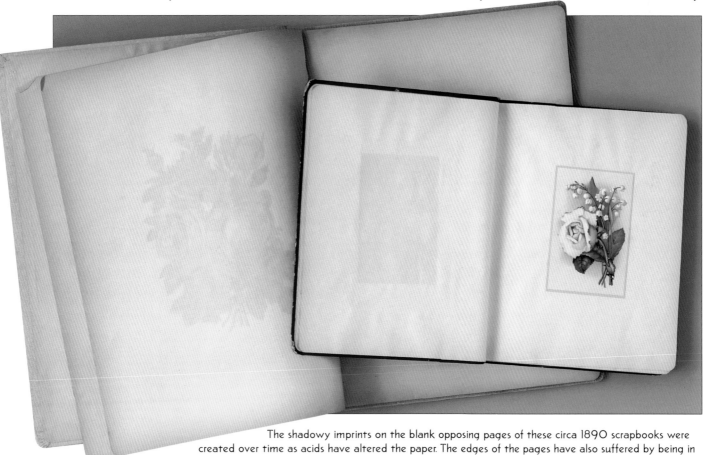

The shadowy imprints on the blank opposing pages of these circa 1890 scrapbooks were created over time as acids have altered the paper. The edges of the pages have also suffered by being in contact with air, light, and atmospheric pollutants.

Many nineteenth-century makers of scrapbooks took pride in their artistic arrangements of ephemera and printed and die-cut "scraps"—and rightly so. Their handiwork survives today as a vivid record of the concerns and lifestyles of a bygone era.

enemies of paper-based products. Lignin, a naturally occurring component of the cell walls of plants, darkens when it's exposed to light. And while the standards for the term "lignin-free" are not as stringent as they are for "acid-free," it's something to consider: Many photo preservationists regard lignin as even more destructive than acid.

OTHER ENEMIES:
LIGHT, HEAT, AND MOISTURE

However you display your photographs and keepsakes or however you store them, the light they are be exposed to will only accelerate chemical reactions that will damage your collections.

Sunlight and fluorescent light wreak the most havoc on your images. Any light will bleach or darken paper, fade ink, change the dyes in color photographs, and cause even black-and-white photographs to grow darker.

While you're probably not ready to turn your house into a mausoleum, you *can* reduce the potential for light damage by taking a few simple steps. First, never leave your book open or on display. Store your photographs and materials in opaque containers or in pH-balanced boxes or folders.

Temperature and relative humidity also affect paper. The more moisture, the faster the deterioration. Paper that is damaged by excessive humidity becomes weak, moldy, and water-stained. Low relative humidity, on the other hand, causes the cellulose fibers in paper to release their water vapor, making the paper dry and brittle and causing photographs to curl. Avoid sudden fluctuations in temperature and humidity, which can cause photo emulsions and ink to crack and book covers to warp.

Set your thermostat at home within an acceptable, consistent range, and keep your archival materials clean and dust-free. This will enable you to achieve the best possible storage conditions. Archival materials should never be stored in an attic, which can be unbearably hot in the summer and frigid in the winter. Basements, often moist and susceptible to leaks and floods, are also bad storage places.

For optimal longevity, every substance in your memory book needs to be taken into account, and every point of contact—paper-to-paper, paper-to-photo, adhesive-to-paper—should be scrutinized for possible adverse reactions.

Carbon-based inks, like those that were widely used before the twentieth century and are still used by calligraphers and artists, are quite hearty. They can withstand most of the ill effects of light, pollution, and humidity. Most modern inks however, do not fare as well. Anything written with an ordinary ballpoint, fountain, or felt-tip pen can be expected eventually to fade, run, and to set off chemical reactions.

Many "acid-free" or "pH-balanced" inks have recently been formulated that have no ingredients that can harm paper or photographs. For scrapbooks, pigment inks are the best choice. Pigments do not penetrate a paper's surface; they cling to it and thus provide a sharper, better-defined line. They also tend to be more resistant to fading. Pigment ink is available in pens as well as in stamp pads that are resistant to light exposure. Both are available anywhere scrapbook supplies are sold.

It's important to pay attention to the adhesive materials you use in your scrapbook as well: Metallic paper clips and staples can mar the pages and will eventually rust; ordinary cellophane tape will cause acid to migrate, will flake away, and will create ugly brown stains; so will most glues. For memory books, photo-mounting squares, paper photo corners, or pH-balanced plastic sleeves can be used for photographs, as can a variety of acid-free, double-sided tapes. Another readily available adhesive is pH-neutral glue which works well with memorabilia other than photographs.

Seriously damaged photographs and documents should be taken to a professional conservator for repair. However, there are some simple situations that you can tackle yourself. If photographs were glued directly onto the book's pages, for instance, you can try to lift the photos off with a microspatula—a special tool with two flattened ends. Slip the microspatula under the edge of the photo and gently move it back and forth. If this technique doesn't work, try cutting away the paper around the photograph. If both sides of the paper have photos on them, you might photocopy the pages onto pH-neutral paper, then store the album, first interleaving the pages with pH-neutral paper, in an acid-free storage box.

Torn documents can be repaired with archival tape by placing narrow strips sparingly on the back. Staples should be removed with a microspatula, one prong at a time, never with a staple remover because they often tear the paper. Slightly curled photographs can be corrected by moistening the backs with a pH-balanced sponge (available at most photography supply stores), placing them between sheets of pH-balanced blotter paper, and weighting the paper down with a heavy object, such as this book, for a couple of days. Recent photographs can be cleaned with non-water-based archival photograph emulsion cleaner, which takes care of soot, grease, adhesive residue, pencil marks, ballpoint ink, and fingerprints. However, none of these techniques should be attempted on old or delicate photographs.

Precious images, such as those shown here, need care that can be achieved only with the use of archival products.

STORING PHOTOGRAPHS

*W*hile inefficient processing methods used by photo labs sometimes leave behind a chemical residue that can cause

photographs to darken, in general, black-and-white images are long-lasting, especially when they are stored carefully. It isn't uncommon for a black-and-white image of an ancestor to have survived—virtually in mint condition—for decades, sometimes even as long as one hundred years.

Color prints are formed through a distinctly different process, one that is, unfortunately, highly unstable. Color photographs are made up of a combination of dyes that fade when exposed to light, with pollution and humidity hastening the process. The dyes hardly ever fade at the same rate, and the result is a surreal kind

Hundreds of interesting products are currently available for creating archival-quality scrapbooks. Rubber stamps, decorative edgers, and other special tools add new dimensions to elaborate layouts.

Sorting and properly storing supplies saves time and money. Shown here is my system for storing the hundreds of ribbons in my collection.

of shift in the color balance. In addition, some prints have a tendency to develop a yellowish cast, even when stored in complete darkness.

So what are we to do? Are all our wonderful photograph albums ticking time bombs? The answer, unfortunately, is yes. The life span of color pictures is so limited that archivists often recommend shooting an occasional roll of black-and-white film to make sure you document the important events and people in your life. It's worth the extra effort. In addition to being inherently more archival, black-and-white photographs have a timeless elegance.

Storing your negatives, while often overlooked, is as important as storing your prints.

Negatives should be removed from the envelopes they come in from the photo shop and placed in chemically stable plastic or pH-balanced paper enclosures. For additional protection, they should be stored in pH-balanced, lignin-free boxes.

Remember to date your photographs as well as you can—the sooner you do it, the easier it is to do, and you will always be grateful for having taken the time needed. Don't use a ballpoint or felt-tip pen: Use a soft pencil, and write on the back of the photograph only, near

many of these protective measures may seem excessive at first, but once you start following these steps they will become automatic. It's not necessary to take an all-or-nothing approach: You may decide to use some archival techniques and materials but that others are too complicated or too expensive for you. That's okay, too. However, once you see the wide range of beautiful archival products that are becoming increasingly available in stores everywhere, you may feel that "partially archival" is not good enough. Most memory books are meant to last because you create them not just for yourselves, but for the benefit of generations to come.

the edges, or make a notation on the outside of the envelope or sleeve in which the photo is stored.

As you extract prints from their envelopes, follow the lead of professional photographers and key the photographs to their negatives to facilitate ordering reprints or enlargements. Easily decoded notation systems are the best—a date plus numbers or letters to indicate a specific roll of film (for example, Christmas '97, roll A). Write the name and number on the back of every photograph from that particular packet, and keep a master list. This may sound like a lot of work, but it really doesn't take that long and can save you hours of frantic hunting for a particular negative later on.

For some of you, particularly those of you who are just beginning your scrapbooks,

DAMAGED PHOTOS

Restoring seriously damaged photographs and removing pressure-sensitive tape should be handled by an experienced conservator. The American Institute for Conservation of Historic and Artistic Works can provide the name, address, and phone number of a conservator in your area.

American Institute for Conservation of Historic and Artistic Works
1717 "K" Street
Suite 301
Washington, DC 20006
Phone: (202) 452-9545

Heirloom or family albums come in all shapes and sizes and can celebrate a single day or an entire lifetime. Shown above are albums capturing the early years of childhood, a memorable family vacation, and a celebration of fifty years of marriage.

SCALING THE FAMILY TREE

Documenting family relationships in a scrapbook may kindle your desire to do an even more extensive search for your roots. Connecting generations, placing each in its own historical context, can bring new life to the names of ancestors that no one really knew or took the time to find out about before.

Creating a genealogy begins at home. Start by making a basic chart with all the information you already have: birth dates and places for you, your parents, grandparents, and great-grandparents, if possible. Check the accuracy of the information with any documentation you have around the house, such as birth certificates and marriage licenses. Then branch out: Old letters, photographs, and family memorabilia can provide additional information and add colorful detail to the stark facts. Be sure to store these documents in a safe place.

Now you can widen the search: Enlist other family members to help provide vital details. Find out where they lived, when and where their relatives were born and died. Show them some of your old photographs and memorabilia in an effort to spur their memories, and ask them to show you any pictures, letters, and the like they may have stored away. An informal approach will be less offputting—people are more likely to open up in a heart-to-heart chat. But always take detailed notes, or if your subject is comfortable with the idea, use a tape recorder. And as you gather information, keep in mind that memory is subjective—just as no two scrap-books of the same event will be the same, two relatives' memories of the same person or event can be as different as night and day.

Record all of your information on standard genealogy forms called *family group sheets*, or *pedigree charts* and be sure to note the source of each piece of data carefully. You can keep the stories, photographs, and other information you are gathering in an ever-growing accordion file. Next, explore local libraries for such items as geographical histories of places where your family members lived. Local courthouses keep records of wills, deeds, and marriage certificates. Newspaper archives and local churches are also invaluable sources of information.

There are scores of genealogical societies and research facilities throughout the country to help guide you in your search. Check your local bookstore or public library for basic "how to" books that outline research methods for trac-ing your own family tree. There are also numer-ous classes available through local colleges and adult education centers. The National Archives

THE UTAH CONNECTION

Utah is, in effect, at the epicenter of the scrapbook-ing explosion that is spreading across the country. Today there are more scrapbooking stores there than in any other state—most probably due to the emphasis Mormons place on family history and genealogy.

Not surprisingly, the state is also rich in resources for researching your family tree—including The Family History Library in Salt Lake, which houses the largest collection of genealogical material in the world. The library, founded in 1894, is dedicated to acquiring and preserving the records not only of Mormons, but of all who care to uncover their roots.

The library sends specialist teams around the world to locate and copy existing records onto micro-film. These films preserve the land grant, deed, parish, will, marriage, cemetery, and other records that docu-ment peoples' lives. Original master copies of the films are stored under carefully controlled conditions in the Granite Mountain Records Vault in the Wasatch mountains southeast of Salt Lake City. This reposito-ry contains a store of about 2 million rolls of microfilm that are safe from flood, fire, earthquake, and man-made disaster. The collection is growing at a rate of more than 4,100 rolls of film a month, and the genealog-ical information can often be accessed at Family History Centers located in Mormon churches around the country—you don't have to make a trip all the way to Salt Lake. For more information, call the Family History Library at (801) 240-1000.

in Washington, D.C., and its twelve regional centers, have census, military, and pension records, passenger and ship arrival logs, plus many more record sources from 1790-1920.

A home-study program, called "American Genealogy: A Basic Course," is offered by the National Genealogical Society in Arlington, Virginia. This course provides information on how to find and use source records, evaluate genealogical evidence, document items, and maintain orderly records.

Because of your efforts, your children will have the privilege of seeing the decades fall away and finding themselves foreshadowed in the eyes of their ancestors.

THE CRAFT OF SCRAPBOOKING

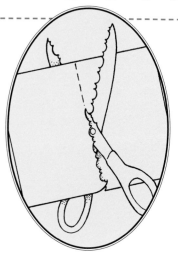

Creating a scrapbook is one of the most powerful ways to celebrate our lives and the lives of loved ones. And the occasions for making a memory album are endless: the joyous birth of a new baby, a romantic, elegant wedding, a long-awaited move to a new house, a fun-filled family vacation, a child's carefree summer at camp, a tribute to a dedicated school group, a pet that's really like a member of the family, and most enduring of all, the preservation of the memory of those you love in a family album that is built over many years. Any event or person close to your heart, any occasion that you especially cherish—all provide perfect reasons to start planning a beautiful, archival album that will ensure that your memories will be preserved for all the years to come.

Before you even begin to approach the construction of a scrapbook, remember this: Enjoy yourself. You don't have to be an accomplished craftsperson to reproduce any of the projects in this book. Don't worry about making your album "perfect." And don't feel that you have to do everything at once. Begin by just getting the photo-filled shopping bags out of the closet one afternoon. That's all. The next day, you can take all the photographs out of one bag and begin to sort them into categories. You can sort pictures by event ("Judy's Wedding," "Our Trip to the Coast," "The Smith Family Reunion") or by subject ("Our New Home," "The Three Jones Sisters," "Angela Learns to Cook," "Mom," "The Elm Street Church Choir"). If you're a photography buff, you might want to organize your pictures into broad categories, such as portraits, landscapes, or animals.

As for the "right time," well, there is no right time. There's only your time. You can designate one day a year for uninterrupted scrapbook making. Or maybe one day isn't enough and you want scrapbook making to become an ongoing part of your life. Perhaps you'll want to set aside every Sunday to do some scrapbooking. Or, who knows? You might be so bitten by the scrapbooking bug that you'll be burning the midnight oil on a regular basis. Everyone has his or her own scrapbooking needs and desires, and you will create a schedule that fits your lifestyle. Whatever your level of interest or enthusiasm, you should congratulate yourself for having gotten the ball rolling.

GETTING ORGANIZED

♦

You can make the task of organizing photos much easier for yourself by establishing an orderly system for storage and maintenance of your pictures. One of the first concrete steps toward creating your own memory book is to sort your photos and memorabilia. The next time you process a set of photographs, instead of storing them in a drawer, put the photographs directly into a book, or any kind of (acid-free) filing system that you have already devised for each important event, member of the family, or subject.

You may already have categories in mind where you feel certain pictures belong—and these categories will most likely end up becoming sections in a book. For instance, if you're documenting a wedding, remember that you will have a certain number of pictures of the rehearsal dinner, some of the ceremony itself, and some of the reception, which will provide natural divisions to your groupings. Other memory books, however, may require a more free-associative approach. If you pull out a shoe box of pictures of your family, there may not seem to be any rhyme or reason to them. But as you look closely, categories will emerge — special places, people, periods, or events. These categories may all fit together under one cover (one page or spread for each topic), or you may want to create a number of smaller books, each with a more specific focus.

The key here, as in all phases of memory-book making, is to allow yourself to be creative in your own, personal way: Go wherever your instincts take you. Once you begin making albums, you'll discover sources of motivation and inspiration everywhere. Many things—from using special scissors to rubber stamps to brightly colored paper—will inspire you in unexpected ways. And that's part of the fun! It's in the process of creating that you will take your greatest pleasure. Just remember, using archival materials now to preserve your work will yield invaluable benefits in the years to come.

SCRAPBOOKING PARTIES

One of the best and most enjoyable ways to tackle the seemingly overwhelming number of photographs you've collected over the years is to organize a scrapbooking party. Your local craft store may offer scrapbooking classes, where you can meet other enthusiasts. Alternatively, you can invite a few of your friends over. Do you know anyone who doesn't have a stash of photographs and memorabilia she'd like to sort through and save? Your party will be an excuse for everyone to get into their closets and emerge with their photos; and the camaraderie that develops when sorting, cropping, pasting, and reminiscing with friends is unique.

While scrapbooking parties are sometimes compared to the quilting bees of old, these gatherings can be even more intimate. Just by surrounding yourself with good friends and treasured photographs, the memories, stories, jokes, and sometimes even tears will begin to flow. Creative scrapbooking suggestions are passed on from one friend to another, along with tips on how to make a scrumptious coffee cake or where to stay in Disney World. Scrapbooking helps us open up to one another; it enables us to share the details—big and small—that are important in our lives.

Scrapbooking with your spouse, parents, and children is a wonderfully familial experience, particularly welcome in this age of overcrowded schedules and fragmented families. The information and knowledge to be gained when your grandmother begins to tell a story, previously unknown to you, about a certain photograph, is priceless. Sharing thoughts and feelings around the scrapbooking table, your family can learn more about each other than in a whole year of Sunday dinners.

If the older relatives can't be there with you, note down some of the things they've told you in the past about places and events, beneath the corresponding photographs. This will be a great gift to your children. And let the kids tell (and write down) their own stories. Your family scrapbook is not just an invaluable heirloom: In the process of making it together, you'll learn about one another and share common experiences. This time together will create its own special memories.

PLANNING AND LAYOUT

How you will tell your story is the great challenge of planning a scrapbook. Scrapbooks tend to flow more seamlessly when there's an underlying reason for the particular layout, something beyond the purely visual. Maybe the album is set up like a time line, telling the sequential story of a family. Or perhaps you'll use your album to document an event, such as a surprise party. You might open the book with a photo of all the hushed partygoers crouched in a darkened room, waiting for the guest of honor. Then, all on a single page: SURPRISE!— a single photo of the awestruck

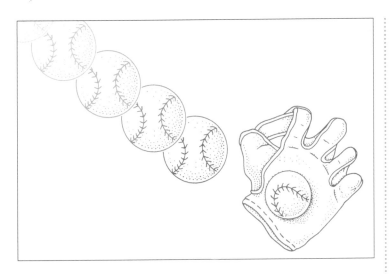

face, colorfully and graphically embellished to reinforce the emotion.

The number of pages in your scrapbook, what those pages will be devoted to, and what style and mood you want to establish are important issues to address when you begin planning your album. Rather than letting the layout of your book just happen, give some time and consideration to your subject; make a plan. There are as many ways to divide your book as there are subjects. The important thing is to know what you will—and won't—include, and to keep that boundary firm. The first half of a memory book on your family history could be about your father and his family, the second half could be focused on your mother and her relatives. For a scrapbook about a summer vacation, you could designate four sections: the trip there, the campground, the lake, and activities in town. Making such decisions beforehand will help you in sorting out your photographs and memorabilia, and once those

choices are made, you can start organizing your decorative materials accordingly—making sure that you won't end up at your final page with nothing but a few bottom-of-the-barrel stickers. And as far as individual pages go, it's usually most effective to have each one focus on a particular event, person, time, or activity. By keeping things focused, you will avoid the kind of haphazard, chaotic page that detracts from the valuable images themselves.

THUMBNAIL SKETCHES

All of the above decisions will determine how your book will flow. What you consider visually important can deliver more impact if it's interspersed throughout the book, rather than being all in one place. One way to ensure this kind of planned progression is to borrow a trick from the magazine and book trades— thumbnail sketches. Make small rough drawings of what every page of the book will include, all set down on a single page so that, at a glance, you have a clear picture of what follows what. The sketches themselves don't have to be detailed; they should provide just enough information to show what will be included. Thumbnails allow you to see the relationship between the pages of your album, giving you a larger view. Rather like visual outlines, thumbnail sketches help you establish the rhythm that will make your scrapbook truly sing.

PLANNING YOUR PAGES

After all the larger decisions as to album type, size, color, and theme have been made, it is time to think of the album's individual pages. Consider all of the following elements when designing your scrapbook.

BALANCE

It is usually best to balance a larger element, on either a single page or a two-page spread, with smaller ones. Arrange all the photographs and memorabilia in a visually pleasing fashion and with a sense that there is a relationship between the two, be it the subject or the mood. Always take care not to make the pages too crowded or too spare. It is usually more effective to have the people in your photographs facing toward you or toward the center of the book—where the eye is naturally drawn—than away from it.

TYPOGRAPHY

Type is a crucial element in the design of any book—memory books included. The right or wrong kind of type and its position on the pages can influence the flow of the book and the way your eye travels over the pages. Type should, like any other design element, fit in with the overall theme of the album, but of course, it plays another crucial role: It provides essential information. If your book commemorates a family reunion, that must be established; key family figures need to be identified, as well as places, dates, etc. Whether written by hand, produced by computer, or created with store-bought lettering, type is a design element that must not only communicate clearly, but will add to the graphic balance of the book.

DESIGN

Plan ahead by beginning to design the style of your scrapbook with the cover. While you can't always tell a book by its cover, a scrapbook's cover is a great opportunity to establish the mood of the interior—theme, color, and texture can all be set up before the first album page is even conceived. You can then use the scrapbook's first single page (before the abundance of two-page spreads) as a kind of title page, rather like the title page of a novel, with the book's subject (or subjects) and author acknowledged.

RHYTHM

There should, ideally, be a rhythm to the way the pages unfold. It is often effective to go from a powerful layout to several calm ones and then back to a powerful one again. Variety is the spice of life, and the drama of difference is what will keep the reader turning the pages with interest.

"WHITE" SPACE

Many an album page has been rendered practically unreadable because the well-intentioned but slightly overzealous scrapbooker didn't understand the power that blank space can bring to a page. As important a design consideration as the photographs and memorabilia themselves, blank or "white" space allows the elements around it to shine. Providing a certain amount of breathing room around your photographs will ensure that they "read" better; it surrounds, it directs the onlooker's focus to a particular face or group, rather than letting them blend in with all the surrounding design elements. Blank space is why artworks or photographs are often matted—surrounded by a wide swath of blank mat board in between the actual frame and the image. This allows the viewer's eye to be drawn to the photo. Blank space lends clarity and heightens impact, all with a minimum of effort. The key is not to be afraid to show a little restraint. While less is not necessarily more in the world of scrapbooking, too much of a good thing can distract from the beauty and wonder of the images the pages are meant to highlight.

MAKING YOUR OWN CHOICES

The important thing to remember when putting together your memory book is that every decision involves an individual choice. Any one material could be used in a multitude of different ways. It's a thrilling moment for any designer when, having made her decisions, she sees how all of her choices suddenly "click" together. Designing is first and foremost a process—you rarely ever know what choice will be the best until you happen upon it, improvising as you go along. Sure, results are important—we all want a memory album that will make us proud, one that will reflect all the time and love that we've put into it. But the discovery that comes with the process, the pure enjoyment of the techniques and materials, is the real thrill of scrapbooking—and of creativity itself.

HOW TO COMPOSE YOUR SCRAPBOOK

The composition of a memorable scrapbook really begins weeks or even months before you actually sit down with your scissors and acid-free glue. It begins with the accumulation of your materials. You needn't restrict your search for materials, such as papers, tools, stamps, stickers, pens, and all the individual trimmings that make your memory book uniquely yours, to a craft, hobby, or art supply store. There are so many interesting elements to scrapbooking available today, you could easily spend the bulk of your time (and money) on expeditions to flea markets, street fairs, museums, or in your own basement or closet—anyplace where the objects that interest and motivate you might be unearthed.

The excitement that comes with the accumulation of materials really intensifies when you allow yourself to be drawn to materials that you might never have considered putting into a scrapbook—the letterhead from a piece of old stationery, an antique paper fan, an origami bird from a child's mobile. The key is to let yourself be as free as possible at first, gathering up all the things that inspire you. Eventually, if you don't already have one, a theme or color scheme will emerge, and your collecting will take on a more distinct focus. You might realize that some of your favorite materials come in shades of gold and ivory—which fit well with your secret desire to create a memory book to commemorate your best friend's wedding. Now, all of a sudden—just as a collector of matchbooks sees matchbooks everywhere she goes— gold and ivory objects, including papers, ink pads, and doilies, will begin to jump out at you from everywhere. You might stumble upon a brass stamping of a cupid, some metallic gold-mesh ribbon, or a handmade bas-relief greeting card with an angel on it, once you have an inkling of your book's subject matter. If you can, collect more than you think you'll need. It's that

great abundance, that gathering of things, that will help stimulate your creativity.

INCORPORATING THREE-DIMENSIONAL OBJECTS

Some of your newfound treasures may be three-dimensional objects, but don't let that discourage you from using them in your scrapbook! Small, interesting objects that can't be attached to the inside pages can be used to decorate the cover of your album to give it charming individuality. Since the outer covers of your scrapbook will never come into contact with its precious inner pages, you can afford to be a bit freer in using these objects—as far as archival considerations are concerned. Color photocopiers are your best bet for bringing three-dimensional objects onto your scrapbook pages (page 67). If photographs are part of the composition, you should anticipate what they may come into contact with before proceeding and take the proper precautions to protect them. Before placing precious old, original photographs into your album, always consider making photocopies of those images on a color photocopier (page 67) and using those copies instead.

If you're creating a memory book based on a specific event, such as a child's birthday, then that occasion will probably be foremost in your mind as you travel through your daily life looking for materials, either deliberately or unconciously. Bright pastels or primary colors will call to you now, and maybe you'll be drawn to objects, such as a little beaded baby bracelet, that you'd never thought of using for the cover of a memory book. Now, somehow, that baby bracelet seems just right.

THE SCRAPBOOK LOOK

········◆········

After subject and color, an overall style is what will make your scrapbook a true attention-getter. You might opt for a contemporary or an old-fashioned look, or a 1950s nostalgic feeling. Whatever design you choose, consistency and a style that is appropriate to the subject you've chosen are the keys to making a scrapbook that tells a story. A memory book decorated with handmade paper is probably more appropriate for a wedding anniversary than it would be to celebrate the first day of school. A bright color scheme with bold lettering and graphics depicting sports equipment would capture the spirit and energy of a ten-year-old boy's birthday party, but a floral theme certainly would not. But while a consistent style is important, it need not be a yoke—the opportunities to be creative within your chosen framework are infinite.

Texture, too, can add tremendous personality to a memory album. Coordinated, compatible textures and patterns add other layers of interest to the story you are trying to tell—and

also a bit of unexpected interest. A book with pages of handmade papyrus would create an intriguing ambience that would add drama to whatever was laid down on its surface. In scrapbook making, as in all things, small decisions can have a huge impact.

Even if you choose only materials and supplies expressly for scrapbook makers—for example, photo-mounting corners that have been laser cut with floral designs—the sophistication of design employed by most of today's manufacturers almost guarantees that your memory book will be beautiful. Merely the wide variety of decorative scissors now available can perform miracles, turning a piece of brightly colored paper into a whimsical frame or border. Indeed, the most basic supplies available in craft shops have a lot to teach the novice scrapbook maker and will guide you to a level of confidence where you will, most likely, want to begin experimenting on your own.

SELECTING A SCRAPBOOK

········◆········

When you're first hit with the irrepressible urge to take photographs and put together a scrapbook, you are faced with two options: You can wander through the aisles of your local craft or paper-goods store for a ready-made album, or you can construct a scrapbook from scratch. If you choose the latter, you'll find some very simple ideas in the following section on how to make your own scrapbook out of wood, paper, or foam board (page 69). While you certainly may be inspired to reinvent the scrapbook from your own point of view, keep in mind that there is a wide variety of albums available today—enough to satisfy everyone's taste, from simple and sedate to wild and whimsical.

Regardless of whether you choose a store-bought album or make one of your own, the one basic requirement that you'll want to keep in mind is that the album be archival.

Among the other issues that will come up while you're planning your scrapbook will be the size of the album: the trim size, the number of pages it might have, and the binding system.

Binding is an important consideration because it will determine whether your album will be restricted to a limited number of pages or whether you can add on as you go along. You may already know, starting out, that you have a limited number of photographs for a particular album, in which case an album with a prede-termined number of pages is fine. You might want to create a number of smaller albums—one for every year of a child's life, for instance—rather than a larger, open-ended volume of the child's early years that can be added to as the need arises.

The binding systems themselves also dic-tate the way the album will lie when opened. Post-bound or permanently bound styles have a tighter spine and will not remain in a flat, open position as easily as the three-ring variety. This may or may not be of concern to you, but, if it

does matter, it's important to take this into account when buying an album. If you've found a book that you love and it has the right number of pages for the materials you want to mount, the issue of how it lies may not be crucial. Three-or five-ring binders (rings with a D shape allow for an even flatter-lying album than those with an O shape), spiral-bound albums, or those with a newer, flexible-strap binding system, do have the advantage of being easier to handle.

As to the type of paper or pages you choose, there are basically two different types of pages available today: the time-honored paper page (albeit acid free) upon which photographs and memorabilia are mounted directly, and the polyester sleeve. The classic sleeve slides over a decorated page, covering it with a chemically stable protective sheet.

Creating your own book, while it takes a bit more effort, has the advantage of being adapt-able to a variety of themes. You can make a heart-shaped book for a wedding album, a base-ball shape for Little League mementos, or even a simple house shape to commemorate the move to your new home.

Whether you buy an album or construct your own, prices range from cheap to dear. Just remember that buying an inexpensive album at a five-and-dime, while it may save you money now, will haunt you in the long run when you're forced to remove your already damaged pho-tographs and memorabilia from their yellowed, acidic pages. Many types of reasonably priced acid-free albums are now available, and spending an arm and a leg for a fancy album doesn't necessarily ensure that it's going to stand the test of time. Just try to keep archival considerations in the forefront of your mind, so you'll be enjoying your handiwork for many years to come.

REUSING OLD ALBUMS

◆

If neither buying nor making a new scrapbook appeals to you, consider refurbishing an old one. Reconstructing an old album can be enormously creative. For one thing, you can make wonderful use of one of those three-ring binders you've kept in your drawer for "whatever," or you can use a child's notebook or a castoff from some completed project. If the cover isn't appropriate for the album you have in mind, you can wrap it in acid-free paper or fabrics to modernize it. Just add endpapers to give it a finished look. Buy new archival pages or make your own to fill the album, and you're ready to begin.

COLOR SCHEMES

It's important to use the colors and materials you're inspired by but also to stay true to a coherent color scheme, be it bright colors, neutrals, pastels, earth tones, or even something as individual as a range of purples. Maintaining a color scheme is the best way to make your album cohere.

Here are a few accepted theories about color that will help you make successful choices.

Colors are often grouped into "warm" and "cool" categories, with the warmest being on the red-yellow-orange side of the spectrum and the coolest being on the blue-green-purple side. Warmer colors, such as yellow, are thought to produce the effect of advancing toward the viewer, while a cool color, such as blue, seems to move away from the spectator—to recede.

Choosing a specific section of the spectrum and sticking with colors from within that section tends to produce a more harmonious feeling than you'd get from an album that's centered wholly on what are referred to as complementary colors, such as orange and blue. Complementary colors are those that are found at the greatest distance apart when the hues are arranged in their natural order around the circumference of a circle, or color wheel.

Of course, the sensory jolt that comes when pairing complementary colors can be used for a special effect—adding a touch of yellow to a page that's primarily turquoise and purple, for instance, makes for a much more complex composition than one that's done only in shades of pink and rose. Just be aware that the color play might upstage your photos and memorabilia.

Our perception of colors also changes as their environment changes—lime green will seem even more vibrant against a dark background than it will against a yellow tone. Outlining something in black will make the color seem even more animated, as a brick wall that's been mortared in white will appear to be of a totally different shade of red from the same bricks mortared in black.

While there are many color theories, there really are no hard-and-fast rules, and interesting combinations abound. We do tend to feel happy when we see bright colors and a bit more calm when faced with blues and greens. And certain colors have longstanding associations (such as purple for royalty, white for weddings, and pastels for babies). There are also colors we are accustomed to seeing together but tend to take for granted, such as the colors of spring or autumn. But whether you choose the colors of your son's baseball team, your house's decorating scheme, or simply your favorite color, success will most likely come from limiting your palette. Choose an array of colors and then use them over and over with slight variations—even combinations as simple as black and white; red, white, and blue; or pinks and purples. Consistency will give your scrapbook an organized, cohesive, and satisfying feel.

CREATING A COLLAGE

The layering of materials is what makes a scrapbook different and infinitely more appealing than the average one-dimensional photo album. While some people feel immediately comfortable with the layering process—often called *collage*—others may be unsure where to start. Here are some simple rules of thumb that will make the planning process a whole lot easier.

WHEN LAYERING, THINK:

············◆············

☞ **BIG TO LITTLE**—It is best to arrange your larger items first, such as a big bright piece of patterned paper or a photo enlargement, with smaller items—frames, lacy doilies, and stickers—relating to them in a large-to-small progression.

☞ **BOTTOM TO TOP**—Choosing the background layers first will ensure that the flow of your album is methodical and appears well thought out. Working from the background layers to the final surface layers will help you to create pages and spreads that really work. Also, by setting out the elements this way first, before mounting, then taking your collages apart and reassembling them, you will avoid any unpleasant surprises. Also see "Making a Collage," page 85.

☞ **PLAIN TO FANCY**—Contrast is what ultimately creates interest on a page. The alternating of a plain background with a fancier embellishment, then a photo, and then perhaps another interesting detail, gives the page more depth and texture.

The beauty of collage is that it is a technique that allows the nonpainter to put together elaborate, dimensional works of art. In the case of scrapbooks, these are truly illustrations, in that they are pictures of something, as opposed to a kind of abstraction. But through the selection and layering processes, anyone at any level of artistic competence has the opportunity and the ability to create intricate, elegant, collaged pages that will complement their treasured memories.

BOX OR SLIPCASE

How will you feel when Junior tips his glass of apple juice onto the precious pages of your family album? Accidents do happen, and one way to be prepared for them is to either make or buy a slipcase for your scrapbooks. A slipcase is a rigid sleeve into which the book slips upright. These are included with some albums or you can make one to fit any album, as shown on page 83.

Experts agree it's best to store books that aren't very fragile in a standing position. But if you want to use a box you already have as an extra bit of protection for your scrapbook, make sure to line it with pH-neutral, buffered paper, and don't place anything on top of the box. Be sure that the book fits easily into the box. There should be just a little space all around, without it being either too big or too small. This will limit the movement of the book in the box and avoid any undue pressure on the book and its contents. Needless to say, your album should now be kept in an especially safe place.

VIDEOTAPING THE BOOK

After you've completed your scrapbook, there may be a long list of loved ones who you know would just love to receive a copy. If, for instance, you've put together a wedding album for the wedding couple, both sets of parents would certainly treasure a copy. Or suppose you've made a family reunion memory book: Wouldn't all members of the immediate family appreciate the time and effort you've put into memorializing the event? One possibility is to request multiple prints from your photo developer and make your albums simple enough that you feel you can comfortably make more than one at a time. (Multiple prints are a good idea in any event—accidents can happen as you're working. You can even make one album for each child and one "family" book, using the same photos for each.) You can also make creative use of a color photocopier (page 67).

Another interesting way of producing more than one copy of your scrapbook, without necessarily working your fingers to the bone, is to use your videotape recorder to make a kind of video book, which can be copied ad infinitum and sent out to every relative on your family tree, if you so desire.

You can use video in a number of interesting ways. One can be just a straight, slow pan of all the pages, perhaps with a quiet piece of music playing in the background. Another option is to include an "insider's" narration of what's going on in the photographs—your own firsthand memories and anecdotes. Someone else in the photo could add his or her personal reminiscences or a number of friends and family can come for a kind of informal interview, talking about their versions of the event, sharing their own impressions and recollections. Through their participation in the process of remembering, a new and richer story might evolve beyond the book's original scope. What results is an even more intimate record—not only of the event that's being set down in the book, but of its creator and perhaps others as well. The video becomes a kind of intimate documentary that not only has the advantage of being archival, but also adds a personal and "you are there" dimension.

COMPUTER TECHNOLOGY

◆

While scrapbooking is largely dominated by simple tools such as scissors and glue—and the application of equal amounts of dedication and elbow grease—it, too, has been touched by the computer revolution. How much technological involvement you want will depend on your level of computer literacy, as well as your access to the hardware and software that can make it all happen.

One of the key ways that computers can serve the scrapbooker is by providing perfect lettering for those who feel their penmanship is inadequate. You can create page titles and photo captions, and print whole pages of your own written text in special creative fonts, just by using software that's compatible with your home computer. Other programs specialize in clip art (or ready-made illustrations)—some offer complex

color images, others simple line drawings. An added plus is that the images can be printed out on pH-neutral paper, with acid-free ink—paste them onto your pages with archival glue and you're set for decades to come. Certain programs also provide various background patterns, so you can print out a page already embellished with design elements, such as angels, paw prints, or ABC designs. These can save the time it takes to decorate a page with things like stamps and stickers.

Other computer software programs even go so far as to enable you to create a kind of multimedia scrapbook on your home computer. These programs allow you to lay out pages on your screen—cutting and pasting your scanned photos and documents with the simple "click and drag" technique familiar to all PC users. You can add decorative borders, clip art, and text to your pages, and then, in a twist that truly takes advantage of computer technology, you can even add audio or video clips. The scrapbook becomes a kind of living document, with a video of the wedding or the brand new baby or a sound bite of your barbershop quartet singing "Sweet Adeline."

Of course, to use any of your photographs in a computer program, they must be converted to or created in a digital format. You can do this either by scanning them yourself (the hardware needed for this has gone down in price dramatically over the past few years), by using a digital camera to begin with (this, unfortunately, is still a rather expensive proposition), or by taking your film to one of a large number of photo developers that will scan your prints onto a computer disc while simultaneously providing you with a set of prints. Either way, you will now have the images in a format that should not fade, yellow, or deteriorate—one of the great advantages to working with a computer. Still, great care must be taken to protect your disc; your challenge will be to make sure it doesn't get lost or damaged. Thinking of it as a treasure as valuable as a family heirloom (you might want to store it in a safe-deposit box or a fireproof safe) will help you take the precautions it deserves. You can even have your photographs developed onto a CD for use in a CD-Rom, enabling you to crop, enlarge, and edit your pictures before printing them out on regular paper or glossy print paper, making as many copies as you wish.

Computer scrapbooking programs aren't necessarily designed to take the place of the physical album we've all grown to cherish. You can still print out your pages and assemble them into a scrapbook that will remain in your living room to show family and friends (as well as allowing you to make numerous copies to send to distant family members). At the same time, you'll know that there is a permanent record on a computer disc that you can even store in a fireproof safe. By taking advantage of computer technology, your memories can benefit from all the protection that the twentieth century has to offer—and you can be assured that they will last well into the twenty-first, if not beyond.

Ultimately, no matter how you create your scrapbook, it will provide endless pleasure for you, your family, and your friends. The following chapter opens a wide variety of design techniques that will help you create unique and memorable albums that will last a lifetime.

SCRAPBOOK MAKING TECHNIQUES

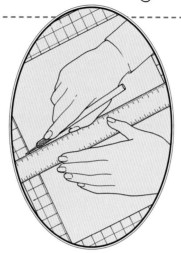

Preserving your memories is easier and infinitely more enjoyable if your workspace, your tools, and your materials are well organized. Planning ahead, making sure you have everything you will possibly need at hand, makes for a relaxing creative experience, as well as a final product that has the finished look treasured memories deserve.

Knowing certain tricks of the trade will also enhance your scrapbooking experience. The following explanations will provide all the information neccessary to tackle everything from our most straightforward album to the more ornate and time-intensive styles. We suggest that you read through pages 39–88 before beginning any project, in order to feel comfortable with the techniques you will be using. We want you to be so confident with your new scrapbooking skills that you will thoroughly enjoy every step—and will be anxious to expand your scrapbooking horizon further and further.

By offering techniques, craft requirements, and information regarding scrapbook making, we also hope to inspire exploration of the creativity that is inside every one of our readers. Our "how-to" section is not as specific as those in many other types of craft books, for we encourage each person to interpret the instructions and adapt them to his or her own personal needs. Our goals are that you become excited by the myriad possibilites inherent in this medium and see scrapbooking as a way of expressing your own artistic spirit, while at the same time connecting with the human need to preserve the memories and mementos that are so dear to us.

Our emphasis in thinking about, designing, and compiling this book has been on the scrapbook as a cohesive unit, rather than on individual pages. We feel that scrapbooks are priceless family and personal heirlooms and that addressing the book as a whole creates an even greater opportunity for one's individuality and creativity to shine forth.

We have presented a designer's "take" on the modern scrapbook and its possibilities. And, as a scrapbook enthusiasts ourselves, we encourage every reader to enjoy and explore this expressive and invaluable tradition.

THE WORKSPACE

Your table can be either stationary or folding; just make sure it's steady, secure, and out of the way of any strong breezes, pets, curious children, windows, radiators, and light sources. If you have the space, it's best to leave the table out, making sure that the items on it are carefully stored when not in use. This way, glues have a chance to dry and ideas have a chance to be born—you are forever able to add an inspired touch to your project. To protect your table, cover it with either a plastic tablecloth or another suitable material. A laminate-topped table that can be folded and easily stored when not needed is not only perfect for making scrapbooks, but also comes in handy when there are extra mouths to feed at holiday time.

There are also those inevitable moments when you'd like to do a little scrapbook work somewhere other than your regular worktable:

in the yard, at a friend's, or in front of the television, for example. Until now it's been difficult to carry all your supplies plus a table of some kind to your workspace of choice, but with the introduction of a number of portable work surfaces, scrapbooking can be as mobile as you are. Some are merely hard, flat surfaces with pillows underneath that conform to the user's lap, while others have been created for craft enthusiasts and have elaborate storage systems beneath the workspace that can be raised and lowered, so that everything from scissors to stamp pads to photographs can be stored and retrieved with ease.

STORAGE

There are certainly no hard-and-fast rules for scrapbooking storage; we're just offering a few tried-and-true suggestions. It's a very individual process—if you find a method or storage solution that works for you, use it. Just remember: Your supplies aren't likely to get damaged or misplaced if you find a specific spot for them and keep them there.

When it's time to put your supplies away, manila envelopes, plastic bins, boxes, and folders all work well—just make sure that every container is clearly labeled. A trip to your local craft or office supply store can yield a wealth of time-saving supplies. The more organized you are to begin with, the less time you'll spend searching for things, and the more time you'll have for actually creating your scrapbook.

Items such as file cabinets (either with or without a top drawer that can store your more bulky supplies) are a wonderful addition to any scrapbooker's workspace. Hanging file folders can put stickers, sheet protectors, die cuts, paper (a folder for each color or type of pattern), templates, and anything else that lies flat at your fingertips, all labeled by the handy tabs at the top. Some are even made specifically for the scrapbooker, with wheels for portability and a case that's designed for small supplies.

While these larger items do involve a bit of initial outlay, rest assured that your money is well spent. Just think of the importance of your project, plus the amount you're spending on supplies that might get damaged if they're not stored properly. You'll also have a much more relaxing scrapbooking experience if you know that there's a place for everything and that everything's in its place.

It is also useful to have a designated box where all forms of scraps and remnants are kept, to be used in a future scrapbook. You can keep paper scraps in various-sized plastic storage bags, each bag designated for a different color. With your box holding all shades of red in one bag and shades of blue in the next, searching for just the right scrap will be easy as thumbing through the phone book. Paper and supplies can be expensive, and it is possible to save lots of time and money by keeping up with your remnants. It is also possible to "see" other projects in the scraps you have left over—some of the most creative albums can be made with leftovers.

Scraps can also be helpful as a potential resource for expanding a single album page into a coordinated two-page spread.

It's also a great time-saver to have a single box that holds all of your most frequently used supplies. This handy container will be the first thing you reach for when you start to work, and you'll be able to leave your less frequently used supplies in their hanging files and boxes, where fewer accidents can happen. It's best to bring these special supplies out only as needed.

Think of your boxes as a giant three-dimensional filing system. If you separate all your hardware into individual categories—for instance: knives, scissors, blades, and punches (i.e. all cutting materials)—you won't waste time looking for things over and over again. Put cutting and punching tools in one container, glues and tapes in another, paint in another and paint applicators in yet another. If you have to combine various types of supplies in one container, be sure to keep the smaller objects divided from the larger ones, or the tiny objects will surely migrate to the bottom, obscured by the larger ones. And always keep your paper products separate from your hardware, or you'll end up with paper that's wrinkled and creased. Many containers are available that are made of either clear or lightly tinted plastic, which makes searching for things much simpler. If your boxes are opaque, just be sure to label the outside of each box. These will be the mainstays of your workspace—an organized and easily accessible place that you have set aside and dedicated to scrapbooking.

It sometimes makes life easier to have containers specifically designated by theme: Halloween, Christmas, Easter, or the beach, for example. Each of these containers can house items that are specific to their category—black cat stickers, punches in the shape of Christmas trees, die cuts of bunnies, even photographs you've set aside for a special page. Then, once you're ready to produce your masterpiece, all your supplies and inspirational materials will be organized, ready, and waiting. You can also use this technique for organizing photographs and memorabilia specific to a single event, such as a vacation to the Grand Canyon. In your well-marked manila envelope, you can keep everything from photos to ticket stubs to the package directions for your freeze-dried camping Chicken à la King. Again, good organization will make your task that much more pleasant when it comes time to actually cut and paste.

Templates can also be stored in a three-ring binder. While they often come prepunched, you can also make the holes yourself. Stickers and die-cut paper shapes can be kept in the 8 1/2″ x 11″ clear plastic pages that kids and other aficionados use to house their card collections. They are available with variously sized pockets that are perfect for whole sheets of stickers as well as smaller quantities.

Archival quality storage boxes are always the best bet for keeping photographs readily available. If you want to move them into other storage containers for a short period of time, while you're working on a particular book, for example, that's OK. Just remember: For the long term, archival is best.

LIGHTING

Lighting should be adequate to ensure accuracy when measuring and to facilitate clean cuts. As mentioned earlier, there should be no direct sun on your workspace, your materials, or your finished product if you want your memories to stand the test of time.

One of the basic principles when compiling and assembling a memory book is that you keep your work surface and, even more important, your hands, clean. Hold photographs by their edges in order to preserve the emulsion, and be sure to clean all ink and glue from your fingers before securing any keepsake to the page. Remember that you are creating an heirloom to pass on to future generations—work with care.

THE BASICS:
WHAT YOU WILL ALWAYS NEED

There are a few basic tools that you should have on hand at all times. Most can be purchased at office or art supply stores, or you may be able to gather them from around the house. Keep the tools readily available, since you will be using most of them for every project in this book. Purchasing good-quality tools and supplies is worth the investment—they'll last a long time, and you won't have to worry

THE BASIC TOOLS

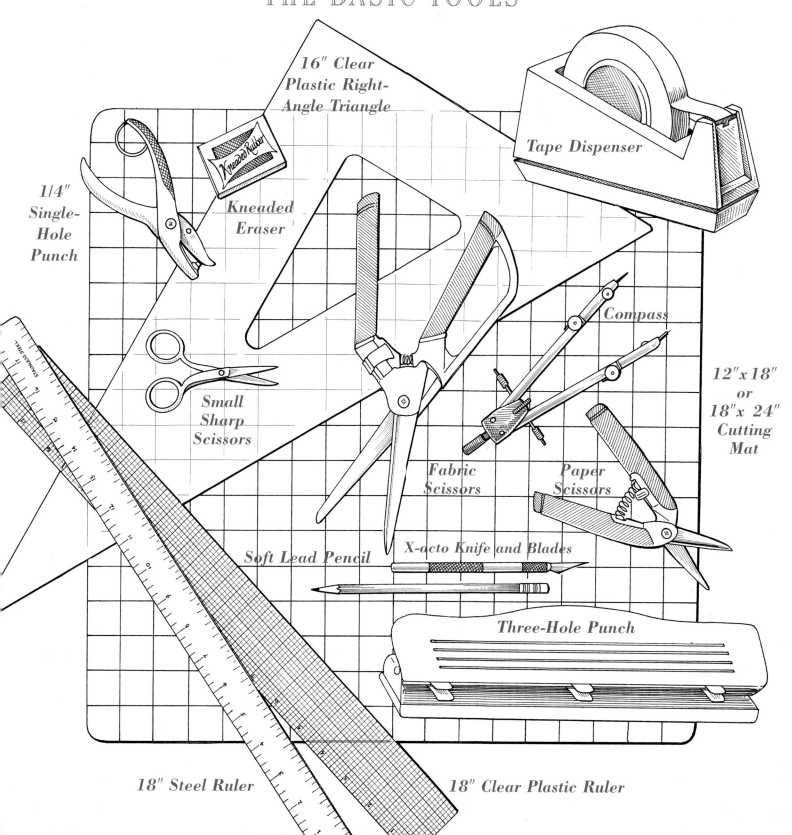

16" Clear Plastic Right-Angle Triangle

Tape Dispenser

Kneaded Eraser

1/4" Single-Hole Punch

Compass

Small Sharp Scissors

12"x 18" or 18"x 24" Cutting Mat

Fabric Scissors

Paper Scissors

Soft Lead Pencil

X-acto Knife and Blades

Three-Hole Punch

18" Steel Ruler

18" Clear Plastic Ruler

about breakdowns mid project or inferior tools ruining your valuable work.

STEEL RULER

A steel ruler is mandatory for precise cutting, and one with a cork bottom is best for cutting with an X-acto knife. The cork bottom prevents the ruler from sliding on the paper. Also, if you are drawing an ink line, the ink won't smear under the edge, because the metal is slightly raised from the surface. A clear plastic ruler helps make measuring easier when working with decorative papers. Always use a steel ruler when cutting with an X-acto knife. Remember: Measurements must be accurate to ensure perfect alignment.

X-ACTO KNIFE

The X-acto knife is used extensively for cutting both paper and mat board. Some people feel more comfortable cutting heavier material with a mat knife; however, if the X-acto is used properly (page 50), it works just fine on all your projects requiring heavier paper or mat board.

BLADES

Use #11 blades for your X-acto knife. They can be purchased in small or bulk quantities, but because it's so important to change blades frequently (to ensure clean cuts and to avoid paper tears), it's best to buy quite a few.

CUTTING MAT

A cutting mat protects your work surface and materials and preserves the blade of the knife. Also, your paper will stay stationary on the mat. Cutting mats are a great time-saver —they ensure accurate cutting of squares and rectangles because of the grid printed on the surface.

TAPE DISPENSER

A tape dispenser allows for one-handed tape use, thus saving time and effort.

TOOLS AND SUPPLIES

- ✻ Steel ruler
- ✻ Plastic rulers and right-angle triangle
- ✻ X-acto knife with blades
- ✻ Cutting mat
- ✻ Removable tape and dispenser
- ✻ Kneaded eraser
- ✻ Scissors
- ✻ Compass
- ✻ Paper punches
- ✻ Acid-free glue and spray adhesive
- ✻ Photo-mount squares
- ✻ Deacidification spray
- ✻ pH testing pen
- ✻ Acid-free pens and markers
- ✻ Pencil, No. 2

KNEADED ERASER

This is a soft, puttylike eraser used to clean your pencil guidelines and tic marks, after the work is completed.

SCISSORS

Skillful cutting is crucial to the overall quality of scrapbooking collage. Small sharp scissors, such as cuticle scissors or small embroidery scissors, work best for curves and intricate cuts. Larger scissors are good for less intricate shapes. It is wise to have an extra pair of scissors to use exclusively for fabric. As you cut, your cutting hand should remain stationary while your other hand feeds the paper. The tip of the small scissors is used for tight spaces and for the tiniest details.

COMPASS

This is a basic tool to have on hand for making circles and arcs.

THREE-HOLE PUNCH

A three-hole punch makes life much easier and saves considerable time when you're making your own 8 ¹/₂″ x 11″ album pages to fit standard three-ring binders and albums.

SINGLE-HOLE PUNCH

Used for making holes for handmade albums, a single-hole punch can also be used decoratively on borders of paper mats, details on corner mounts, and directly on your album to create unique border effects. In addition to a standard-size punch, look for hole punches in different sizes and shapes to decorate with, such as the tiny heart-shaped punch that we have used on several projects.

RIGHT-ANGLE TRIANGLE

Made of clear plastic and used to draw squares and rectangles, this tool simplifies a variety of cutting tasks. Because it's clear, it makes cropping photos, decorative papers, etc., easier.

SUPPLIES AND PRODUCTS

The supplies and products we're recommending here are those we used extensively in the studio as we have created projects for this book. We've tested other products and can say that the ones we've chosen should perform well for you. Most are readily available at craft and art-supply stores or through mail-order sources.

NEUTRAL-pH ADHESIVE

An acid-free white glue used for paper and board that dries clear and remains flexible, it can be applied easily with a brush and cleans up with water. It is ideal for small pieces of paper, but do not use on photographs. Manufactured by:

Lineco Inc.
Holyoke, MA 01041
(413) 536-6061

Zig is the Millennium, which is also acid free and available in several colors. Manufactured by:

Kuvetake Co. Ltd., Japan
E. K. Success
P.O. Box 6507
Carlstadt, NJ 07072

DEJA VIEWS

Plastic shape and border templates are ideal time-savers for creating distinctive shapes and edges. Manufactured by:

The C-Thru Ruler Co.
6 Britton Drive
Box 356
Bloomfield, CT
(860) 243-0303

RUBBER STAMPEDE®

A wide selection of images are available on fine quality rubber stamps, including Cynthia Hart's Victoriana Collection. Use with acid-free stamp pads and stamp cleaner. Also available are:

DELTA DECORATIVE STAMPING PAINT
One of the best-quality paints created for stamping fabric, paper, walls, and wood, it is water-based, acid free, and easy to clean up.

RUBBER STAMPEDE™ DECORATIVE STAMPS
Dense foam stamps that are excellent on paper when used with Delta Stamping Paint and that can also be used on walls, furniture, and fabric. Manufactured by:

Rubber Stampede
Berkeley, CA 94701
(800) NEAT FUN

"SCRAPBOOK WORKSHOP" PRODUCTS

Cynthia Hart's fabric scrapbook craft panels and 100 percent cotton fabrics by the yard are manufactured by:

V.I.P. Fabrics
469 Seventh Avenue
New York, NY 10018
(800) 847-4064

Cynthia Hart's scrapbook papers, stickers, and binders are manufactured by:

Frances Meyer Inc.
P.O. Box 3088
Savannah, GA 31402
(912) 748-5252

Cynthia Hart's Family Scrapbook Calendar is published by:

Workman Publishing
708 Broadway
New York, NY 10003

TIPS AND TRICKS

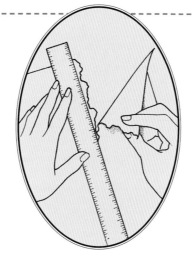

READY REFERENCE TIPS AND TRICKS

◆

How to Enlarge or Reduce a Pattern
or Template with a Copier 50
How to Cut Cardboard and Paper................50
How to Apply Glue with a Brush 51
How to Iron Paper 52
How to Cover a New Notebook
or Album................52
How to Cut Your Own Album Pages 54
How to Make Spacer Strips 55
How to Use Protective Sleeves................56
How to Create a Random-Torn Edge 56
How to Use Decorative Paper Edgers................57
How to Use a Decorative Paper Punch................59
How to Make a Paper Corner Mount 61
How to Make Paper-Cut Designs 63
How to Cut a Stencil................64
How to Stamp Single- and Double-Imprint
Designs................64

How to Crop a Photograph................65
How to Make a Photo Cropper................66
How to Use Color Photocopying 67
How to Include Journal Entries and Titles 68

MAKING YOUR SCRAPBOOK

◆

The Basic Book................69
The Traditional Book 72
The Laced Scrapbook................74
The Wood Books................78
The Foam Board Books................80
Storage Containers for Your Scrapbooks................82

MAKING A COLLAGE

◆

Basic Steps................85

HOW TO ENLARGE OR REDUCE A PATTERN OR TEMPLATE WITH A COPIER

The easiest way to enlarge your pattern or template is with a photocopier with an enlarging capability. Place the book directly onto the copying machine to enlarge. If the book does not lie flat enough, you can eliminate any resulting distortion by tracing the pattern onto tracing paper first, and then photocopying the tracing.

To photocopy the pattern in the same size as the printed pattern, you need to set the copier (or ask the operator to set the copier) at full size—in other words, at 100 percent. To enlarge or reduce the picture, you need to know the percentage of enlargement or reduction necessary to give you the final size you want. Use the following formula, in which X equals the percentage of change needed:

$$X = \frac{100\% \text{ x final size desired}}{\text{size of printed pattern}}$$

For instance, if the printed pattern is 6 inches wide and you wish to enlarge it to be 9 inches wide, use the formula:

$$X = \frac{100\% \text{ x } 9}{6}$$

$$X = \frac{900\%}{6}$$

$$X = 150\% \text{ enlargement}$$

If you wish to reduce a printed pattern that is 8 inches wide to make it 5 inches wide:

$$X = \frac{100\% \text{ x } 5}{8}$$

$$X = \frac{500\%}{8}$$

$$X = 62.5\% \text{ reduction}$$

Once you have enlarged your pattern to the desired size, cut out the shape and trace it onto the decorative paper you wish to use. With scissors, carefully cut out the shape.

HOW TO CUT CARDBOARD AND PAPER

Start with a sharp new blade in your X-acto knife and a cutting mat. Practice first on scrap paper. Measure and lightly pencil-mark a cutting line. Place the ruler along the cutting line. With your fingers, firmly press down to hold the ruler in position, keeping your fingers safely away from the very edge to avoid cuts. To cut through foam core board or mat board, lightly score the cutting line with your X-acto knife,

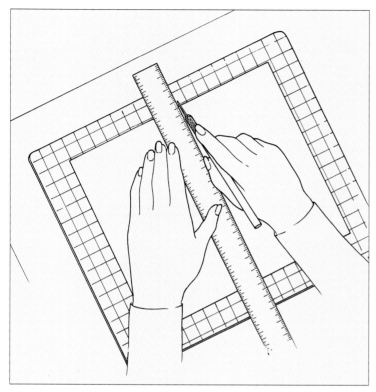

Cut along ruler edge with X-acto knife.

then retrace the line lightly with the knife two or three times more to make a clean cut. For a long cut, make several even strokes with your knife to ensure a straight, clean line; do not try to make the cut in one stroke because your hand will ultimately waver and make the blade go off the line. The trick is to be steady, making firm but easy strokes.

Practice using the same technique on card stock. Two strokes with the X-acto knife should make a clean cut. For stationery-weight paper, one stroke should be sufficient.

Whenever possible, cut on the outside edge of the cutting line (toward the part to be dis-

carded), so that if the knife slips, you will not damage the art or photograph.

HOW TO APPLY GLUE WITH A BRUSH

Many of the collage pieces in this book are adhered with glue applied with a brush (see "Scrapbook Designs"). An acrylic brush, or any inexpensive brush of the right size will do. The size of the cut-out determines the size of the brush to be used. A number 6 brush is a good size for most projects, and smaller brushes—numbers 2 or 3—are good for pieces less than 1 inch in size.

Keep a glass of warm water with a drop of dishwashing liquid in it at hand to soak the brush when not in use. Dry the brush with a rag or paper towel before use. You never want to place a wet brush in the glue because it will dilute the glue and possibly cause your paper to buckle. Dip the brush into the glue and wipe the excess off against the rim of the glue container. Do not overload the brush. The glue should be applied in even strokes; cover the entire piece to be glued with a thin coat. Position the piece to be glued and gently press it in place. Carefully blot any excess glue off with a cloth. We use a neutral-pH adhesive for most projects, especially on the smaller paper pieces; it is a water-soluble adhesive, so that if you don't like what has been glued down, you can lift it off again by wetting it.

Remember to replace the cap on the glue container after use, and wash your brush thoroughly. If the glue should thicken or dry out, it can be thinned with a little water to its original consistency. If you use the glue as suggested, you should have no buckling. However, should there be any buckling or waviness after you have adhered the collage pieces to your paper, put the paper between two sheets of wax paper and weight it with a heavy book. This will flatten the paper almost entirely. It is best to avoid this problem by carefully applying a light and even amount of glue to your collage pieces.

An alternative glue is Yes!, a gel paste that can be thinned with water and applied with a small sponge brush. Spread on the glue in an even coat with the consistency of rubber cement. It will dry to a clear finish. This glue works well for both small paper pieces and large ones. When you are finished working, be sure to clean your brush with warm, soapy water, and rinse well.

How to Iron Paper

Your projects may include paper memorabilia such as maps, brochures, itineraries, cards, and notes. If these items are wrinkled or creased, you may wish to iron them before arranging them in your book.

Lay the item, face down, on the ironing board and cover it with a layer of plain white paper. With a dry iron set at the lowest temperature setting, iron it gently. To get rid of more stubborn wrinkles, increase the temperature slightly and test-iron a corner to see if the paper can withstand the heat without scorching. After ironing on one side, flip the paper over, cover again with a layer of paper, and iron the other side.

How to Cover a New Notebook or Album

The post scrapbook is the most readily available basic scrapbook album. The two posts unscrew, allowing you to remove the posts, cover boards, and album pages. You can then cover the boards and reassemble. Three-ring binder notebooks are also readily available, relatively inexpensive, and come in a variety of sizes. Some are padded, making them particularly desirable for covering with fabric or with medium-weight, textured, handmade papers. Remember: When you choose a cover paper, avoid thin papers, such as tissue paper, which tears too easily, or thin gift wrap, which bubbles and wrinkles easily. If you plan to cover a dark-colored binder or album, overlay the outside of the cover boards with white paper first, before you use your special fabric or paper. The following technique can be used for all sizes and types of binders:

Cut out the cover fabric or paper $1^{1}/_{2}$ inches larger all around than the binder when opened flat. (If the book has a curved spine, cut the fabric or paper $1^{1}/_{2}$ inches larger at the top and bottom and 2 inches larger at the sides.)

Center the book on the cover piece. Check that the cover will fit when the binder is closed.

For binders and albums with square corners, use scissors to clip the corners at a 45° angle, cutting 1 inch beyond the corner, and make two vertical slits at the top and the bottom of the binder spine.

Following the manufacturer's directions, apply spray adhesive to the wrong side of the cover. With the binder folded, center the binder on the cover and press down gently, making sure that there are no bubbles or creases along the spine. Then smooth the cover over the front and back boards of the binder.

Following the drawing, open the binder flat, fold up the tabs at the top and the bottom of the spine, and glue them in place at the ends of the metal strip. At each corner, fold the diagonally cut edge over the corner of the board. Then neatly fold the cover flaps over the side edges of the binder and press them in place; fold and press the top and bottom cover flaps in place, making crisp, neat corners.

Use fabric, rather than paper, to cover binders and albums with rounded corners. Cut the fabric with rounded corners, keeping the excess fabric an even 1½ inches all around. First fold the top, bottom, and side flaps of the fabric

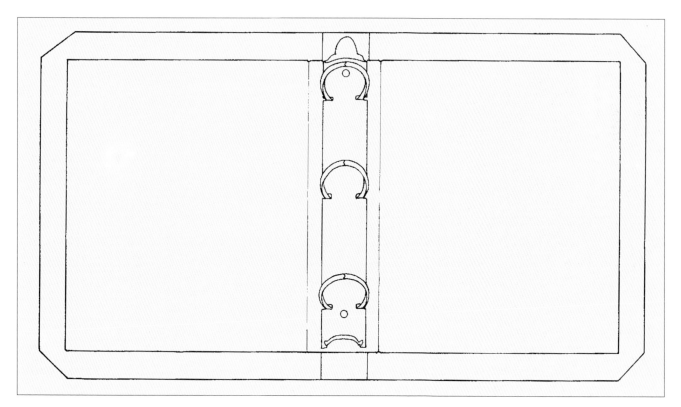

Trim cover fabric or paper 1½" larger than opened binder. Trim at corners as shown.

cover over the edges to the inside, leaving fabric at the corners extending outward. Then, at each corner, make tiny gathers or tucks to distribute the excess fabric evenly and neatly around the corner. When you add the liner pieces, round the outer corners of the liner to keep it an even $1/2$ inch smaller than the cover edge.

Measure the binder boards, then cut the inside liner (end) paper or fabric $1/2$ inch smaller at the three outer edges for the front and back. Use spray adhesive on the wrong side of the liner and adhere to the inside of the binder front and back, butting one edge up against the metal spine and letting the other edges overlap the cover flaps.

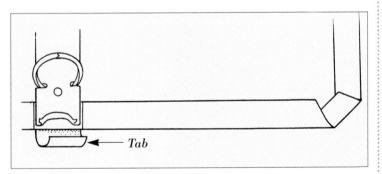

Fold up tabs at top and bottom of spine.

HOW TO CUT YOUR OWN ALBUM PAGES

Most notebook ring binders come in a standard size, using $8\frac{1}{2}'' \times 11''$ filler paper. This makes filling your book easy. Solid-colored, acid-free stationery in this size is available either in packages or by the pound. All you have to do is punch the holes with a three-hole paper punch.

If you plan to use an empty post album without pages included, you have the choice of buying packaged pages or making your own pages. To make your own pages, cut paper to a size $1/4$ inch smaller all around than the album cover. With a single-hole paper punch, make holes that correspond to the album posts. You can make pages this way for any size rectangular album (purchased or self-made), punching the holes where needed to attach them to the album covers.

If you have a special-shaped book that uses rings or album posts to attach the pages to the cover, such as the Wood Heart Book (page 109),

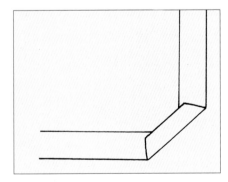

Fold diagonally-cut edge over the corner of the board.

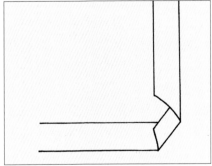

Fold cover flaps over the side edges of the binder.

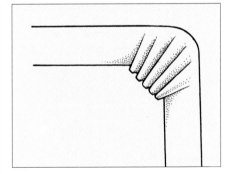

For rounded corners, gather excess fabric.

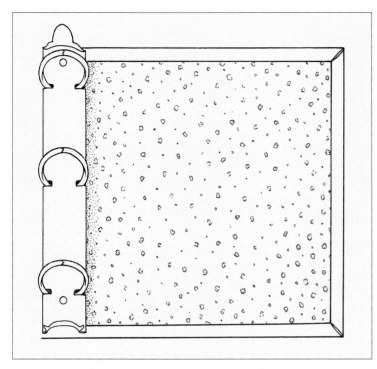

Glue liner to hide cut edges of cover flaps.

that are given in the individual book directions.

For more complicated shapes, such as the Horse Book (page 172), with pages attached directly to the cover, use the pattern as a template (these pages are the same size as the cover) to cut album pages from black paper. To join the pages, lay two pages (flipping one page over) side by side with the straight portions of the sides just touching; cut a strip of black tape to fit and press it down along the seam. Fold the pages together along the seam with the tape inside. Join another pair of pages the same way and fold them together. Then lay the two folded pairs together with the seam edges touching; tape them together and fold. Add more pages in the same manner, if desired. Work carefully, always making sure the shaped edges match each other (if necessary, trim with an X-acto knife). These pages are tied to the cover as in the case of the Traditional Book (page 72).

HOW TO MAKE SPACER STRIPS

To allow for the thickness of the collage layers and memorabilia you wish to add to your album, you can make spacer strips to go between your album pages.

Use acid-free mat board, or, for very thick pages, foam core board, $1/8$ inch or $3/16$ inch thick. Cut the strips the same height as the album pages and the width needed to reach from the edge of the album page to at least $1/4$ inch beyond

first make a template to cut out the pages. Use the pattern that you used for the cover to draw the shape onto paper. Then, at the outer edges, draw another line $1/4$ inch in from the outline, following the contours of the shape. At the edge where the pages are to be attached to the cover, make the page the same size or only slightly smaller to allow enough room for the holes. (There should be at least $1/4$ inch between the page edge and the holes to ensure that the pages will be strong enough to withstand wear.) Cut out the template and use it to cut out the shaped pages to fit your book. With a single-hole paper punch, make holes to correspond to the cover holes. Be sure to follow any special instructions on making pages

the holes, or for a traditional scrapbook, the same width as the binding strips. Punch holes in the strips to correspond to the holes in the album pages. Insert the spacer strips, alternating them between the album pages.

One place you want to be sure you use spacer strips is in books where small foam disc mounts are used to give a 3-D look to the pages. You can also use small pieces of scrap foam core board, mat board, or even bits of cosmetic sponge to elevate pieces. Whatever you use, the spacer strips will separate the pages to allow for this added thickness.

HOW TO USE PROTECTIVE SLEEVES

To protect special heirloom photographs or fragile decorations, such as the paper-cut work in the Dog and Cat Books (pages 174 and 177), insert the pieces into protective sleeves, which can be purchased. Intricate cover decorations, as on the Baby Book (page 110), should also be protected by a sleeve, since the ornaments are exposed and therefore especially vulnerable.

The sleeve should fit the album piece it is to protect rather snugly, yet be loose enough for slipping in the material without doing any damage. You can make your own sleeves (or cut down the packaged ones) to fit special-sized pieces by cutting a piece of lightweight acetate to the width of your material and

a length 1 inch more than twice the length. To make the sleeve, fold one length to the back, and with this fold at the bottom, fold the top 1 inch to the back, leaving one plain length as the front of the sleeve, with the top inch overlapping the back length.

In addition to protective sleeves, you can purchase protective sheets to place between your album pages to keep the facing-page decorations from catching and tearing.

HOW TO CREATE A RANDOM-TORN EDGE

The torn edge gives an interesting custom-made look to your scrapbook. To create a torn edge and still have the paper be squared is easier than you may think. Measure and light-

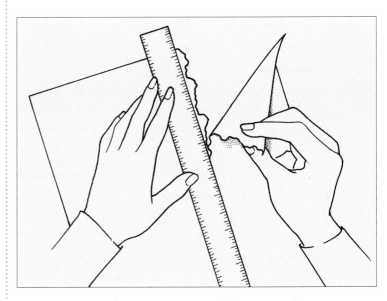

Gently tear away excess paper using ruler as a guide.

ly pencil-mark your paper, leaving 1 inch or more along the edge to be torn away. Place a steel ruler along the pencil line, holding it firmly in place, and tear away the excess paper, pulling the strip gently to the right and left as you tear, using the ruler as your guide.

How to Use Decorative Paper Edgers

Paper edge scissors (paper edgers) that make decorative cut edges are available in craft stores; they are similar to pinking shears used in sewing. The paper edgers come in several cutting patterns, and they can be used by right- or left-handed people. They can even be used upside down to create a reverse-pattern edge.

To make a simple straight-cut edge, draw a straight line with a pencil and ruler, then cut along the outside of the line so that the shaped edge of the top blade falls just along the line (page 58). Each time you shift the blade to cut farther, be sure to match the blade to the previously cut edge so that the pattern continues smoothly.

To make a symmetrical edge (as for a photograph frame), first make a template of the cutting pattern, using card stock and cutting it a little longer than you will need for your project. On the paper rectangle for your project, center the template along the planned border edge so that the cut pattern will end at a corresponding point at each corner to create matching corners.

If your scissors have a pattern that is asymmetrical, simply match the corners as closely as possible. Lightly draw the border onto the rectangle. Repeat along each remaining border edge, centering the template each time. The top and side edges do not have to be identical at the corners, but they should form a consistent corner treatment for all four corners (page 58).

Cut out, carefully matching the scissor-blade design to the marked border edge.

To cut an opening at the center of a rectangle, measure and pencil-mark the desired edge of the opening. Center your template along one edge of the opening, matching the inner (deepest) part of the cut design to the line, with the rest of the cut edge extending into the opening. Pencil-draw the border edge.

Repeat along each remaining edge to the opening, making all four corners as consistent as possible. With regular scissors, rough-cut away the opening center, leaving the marked border edge. Starting at the center of one edge, clip to the marked line, and matching the blade design of the paper edger to the marked border edge, cut the border to the corner. Then, holding the paper edgers upside down, if needed, to reverse the design, cut the marked edge from the center to the opposite corner. Repeat on each edge around the opening. See the drawing on the next page. (If your cutting pattern is asymmetric, you will need to make the entire cutting for each edge in the same direction.) If necessary,

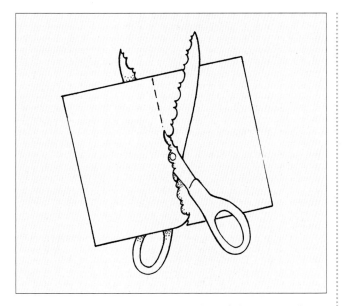

Cut along the line, matching the edge of the paper edger blade to the line.

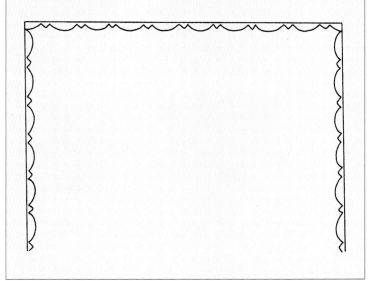

Center the cutting pattern along each edge to form uniform corners.

use regular scissors to make a diagonal clip in each corner to make it easier to position the paper edger to cut the border design near the corners. Use an X-acto knife to correct any uneven cuts. Flip the cut paper over to use the unmarked reverse side as the right side.

You can also use your paper edgers to cut thin strips of colored paper to decorate your album. The same paper edger can cut strips with different looks by cutting both edges the same way; or by cutting the second edge with scissors turned upside down to reverse the pattern; or by cutting one edge in one direction and reversing it for the other; or by staggering the spacing of the pattern on the edges. Varying the width of the strips also changes the look. Practice on scrap paper to discover the possibilities for the particular pattern of your paper edgers.

In addition to the paper edgers that cut decorative straight edges, there are also special paper edgers to cut decorative corners, either convex or concave, depending on how you hold the scissors.

There are hand-held rotary cutters with interchangeable blades for cutting decorative edges; they are easy to use if you cut with the blade following a thick straight edge. Also available are special paper cutters that have interchangeable blades to cut decorative edges; they are useful if you plan to cut large quantities of strips and fancy edges.

To make large-patterned edge decorations (larger than possible with the paper edgers), use the plastic templates for decorative edges readily available in craft stores. Place the decorative edge of the template along the edge of your project, centering it as with the paper-edger template, and draw along the template edge to mark the design on your paper. (Work on the underside of the paper, if possible, so the markings won't show on the finished project.) With an X-acto knife, carefully cut along the marked design edge.

A plastic template can also be used as a stencil (or to make a longer stencil from acetate, see page 64) to add a decorative colored border to a rectangular mat opening or the outer frame edge. Simply center and position the template or stencil about ¼ inch from the straight edge to be bordered, with the patterned edge facing toward the border area. Paint or color with markers the border area between the template and the straight edge.

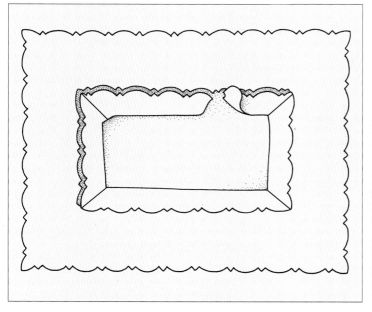

Rough-cut out the center opening, then use edgers to cut the border along the edge of the opening.

HOW TO USE A DECORATIVE PAPER PUNCH

Decorative paper punches, available in craft and art stores, are small circular or rectangular devices that feature a bottom slot to position the paper edge and an easy push button to punch out the indicated shape.

To position the paper punch-out correctly, remember that the cutout will be directly under the push button, as indicated, and the center of the punch-outs can be positioned no more than about 1 inch in from the paper edge. Practice on scrap paper to see how your punch works, and then take the time to measure and plan the placement on your project.

To create an even border along the edge of the paper, mark the center of the paper edge and center the punch over the mark. Push the paper into the bottom slot of the punch as far as it will go. Mark a light pencil guideline along each side of the punch, then make your punch-out.

Move the punch to the left, lining up the right edge of the punch with the previously drawn guideline. Draw a new guideline along the left side of the punch, then make your punch-out. Continue working to the left, lining up along the old guideline, drawing a new guideline, and punching out evenly spaced designs. Then start at the center punch-out and work to the right. You can use the punched-out shapes

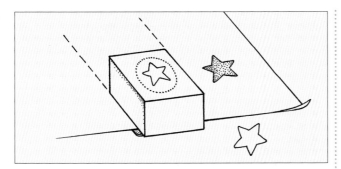

Move the punch along the paper edge, marking and following the guidelines to position designs evenly.

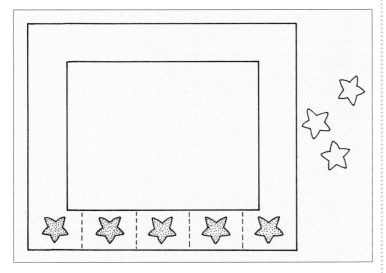

Punch out evenly spaced designs, saving the punched-out
shapes for later use.

as additional decorations in your album.

To position punch-outs more (or less)
widely spaced, determine how many punch-outs
you want along the edge. Mark the center of
the paper edge, and working outward, measure
and lightly mark the position for the center of
each punch-out. Determine the center of your
punch and mark it, if it is not already marked.
Match the center line of the punch to the pen-

ciled mark and punch out the shapes. You can
use this method to punch directly onto the
page edges of your album.

In addition to page borders, you can
make decorative frames for your photographs.
Cut a rectangle 1¼ inches (or more) larger all
around than the photograph, cutting the edges
with a paper edger (page 57). Planning placement, punch out a star at each corner and alternate hearts and circles (made with a single-hole
paper punch) along each edge between the
stars. Back the frame with contrasting colored
paper, if desired.

Cut a heart-shaped frame and punch
evenly spaced circles or hearts around the
frame.

Cut a rectangular frame for a photograph. Decorate it by punching out a heart at
each corner, then use a corner punch to cut the
scalloped corner design.

Trim album pages with punched-out design along the
edge.

Punch designs in photograph frame and back with colored paper.

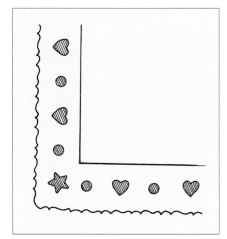

Cut a heart-shaped frame and punch out designs all around.

Punch out designs just at corners for rectangular frame.

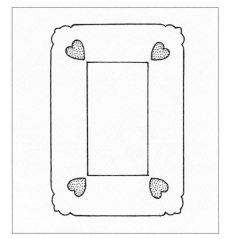

HOW TO MAKE A PAPER CORNER MOUNT

BASIC DIRECTIONS

Trace the pattern and cut it out. Draw the pattern on card stock. Cut out the complete shape, then cut away the outer corner, if desired, or make a decorative edge (follow directions).

Fold squares A and B under the corner (C) section; glue squares A and B together to complete the corner mount. The photograph will slip under the open corner section.

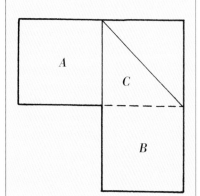

Fold squares A and B under C to form corner mount.

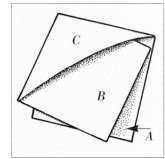

DECORATIVE CORNER EDGES

1. To use a decorative paper punch (page 59), first punch the shape out of the card stock, then position and draw the pattern around the hole, so that the cutout is centered at the outer corner of section C.

HOW TO CUT A STENCIL

Many materials can be used for stencils. A very good one is .01-weight clear acetate, available in pads, rolls, or sheets at art-supply stores and some craft suppliers. Although lighter weights are often recommended for cutting curves, the heavier weight is more durable and less likely to tear with use.

Trace your pattern onto paper. Lay a piece of acetate, cut 2 inches larger all around than your pattern, over your pattern, and securely tape them together to prevent shifting. With a ballpoint pen, trace the design onto the acetate. If your stencil design is simple, with only one or several scattered openings, you are ready to cut. However, if your design is more complex, with several openings close together, you need to plan "bridges" between the openings to keep the center portions of the stencil intact.

Place the acetate on a cutting mat and cut out the stencil openings with an X-acto knife. Now your stencil is ready.

Use acrylic paint for paper and fabric paint for fabric. For small projects, a sponge or a sponge paintbrush make the application of the paint easy. Dampen the sponge or paintbrush and squeeze out any excess water. Dip into the paint and test-paint, with a dabbing motion, on a piece of scrap paper. The paint should be neither too heavy nor too light. Excess paint on the applicator can be dabbed off on a paper towel. Practice until you can judge when you have just the right amount of paint on the applicator.

Place the stencil on the item to be stenciled, and without shifting it as you work, apply paint through the stencil openings. Remove the stencil, carefully lifting it straight up, and allow the project to dry. To prevent smudges, wipe the underside of the stencil clean and be sure it is dry before reusing.

HOW TO STAMP SINGLE- AND DOUBLE-IMPRINT DESIGNS

We used a foam-surfaced design stamp and stamping paint to make a more richly textured imprint than rubber stamps used with an ink pad make. Be sure to practice on scrap paper until you can achieve the desired effect, before imprinting your project.

Position the dry stamp as desired on the paper. Lightly pencil-mark the position of the stamp. Repeat for each place you plan to imprint the design, spacing any repeated designs evenly over the paper. With a fine-textured foam cosmetic sponge, apply a light coat of the stamping paint to the design surface of the stamp, covering the whole surface with a light, but even coat. Be sure to cover just the surface of the stamp; paint in the recesses of the design may print a glob of excess color.

For a single imprint, using your penciled marks as a guide, position your stamp and carefully make the imprint on the paper, lowering the stamp straight down and raising it up from the paper without any sideways movement that will cause a blurred imprint.

Add fresh paint for each imprint, making any additional imprints as desired. When you are finished, clean the sponge and the stamp surface with lukewarm soapy water; rinse and blot dry with a paper towel.

With the foam stamp, you can use more than one color in a single imprint by sponging different colors on separate sections of the stamp design, and then making your imprint. For an example of this technique, see the pink rose with green leaves in the Windows on the Past album, (page 102).

For a double-imprint design, use the light-colored paint first. Position your stamp about ⅛ inch to one side of your pencil-marked ticks, and print the design for the first (shadow) imprint. Adding fresh paint for each imprint, stamp all the planned first imprints in this manner. While these first imprints dry, clean the sponge and the stamp surface with lukewarm soapy water; rinse and blot dry with a paper towel.

When the first imprints are completely dry, apply the dark stamping paint to the stamp surface with the sponge, and, following the pencil marks exactly, stamp the second (main) imprint, so that just a shadow edge of the first imprint shows around the second one. Repeat until all designs are double-imprinted. Clean your tools as before.

For the Windows on the Past album, we used rubber stamps and colored ink pads, as well as the foam stamps. Always remember to lower and raise the stamp directly without any sideways movement, to prevent blurring. To ensure perfect results, you can always stamp the designs onto separate pieces of paper, then cut them out and attach them where you wish. This allows you to discard any blurred imprints and to position the imprint exactly where you want it to go. You can stamp the designs in one color and fill in the design with colored pencils or markers.

How to Crop a Photograph

Cropping involves cutting away what you consider to be unnecessary space or extraneous details around the subject of a photograph. In doing so you are helping the eye to focus on what's truly important—by getting rid of all (or at least some) distractions the picture's essence emerges. But while many snapshots taken in the haste of a photogenic moment need a little help, it's also important to remember that many a well-intentioned scrapbooker has become a bit too "crop-happy," and actually lessened the impact of their photographs.

The first thing to remember when cropping is that it's always a good idea to have duplicate photos. That way, if you make a mistake, it's not irreversible. Next, take a good long look at your pictures. Try to determine if the details you are thinking about cutting away add to or detract from the story of your photograph, as well as the story of the page you're putting together. You may want to have a heart-shaped closeup of the bride and groom. On the other hand, details such as the wedding cake, her dress, the outdoor scenery, and the "getaway car" may serve as treasured reminders of the day in the years to come, and may be best left in. Often it's best to leave a number of photographs in their original shapes, and use the cropped images as accents.

Once you've decided that you want to crop, try to chose a shape that enhances your picture and the story behind it. There is a wide variety of tools to help you create a unique shape—clear plastic templates that you can buy are great because you can see exactly what you're cutting out and what you're leaving in. However, you can make your own photo croppers. Here are a few tips for making a cropper for any size or shape photograph.

How to Make a Photo Cropper

This nifty trick will ensure perfectly cropped (cut) photographs. Place a piece of acetate or a sturdy clear plastic bag over graph paper or a grid (such as on your cutting mat). Use the underlying grid for a measurement guide, and with a ballpoint pen, mark the corners for a rectangle (or a square or diamond) of the desired size. With a steel ruler and the pen, draw the connecting lines between the corner marks to complete the rectangle to be used as a window for cropping.

For rectangles, slip the photograph under the marked shape on the acetate, and position it within the outlined window just as you want it to be cropped. Without shifting the position, use a pin to pierce each corner of the shape, pushing the pin straight down through the acetate and the photograph at the very corners of the outlined window. Remove the acetate. Flip the photograph over. On the reverse side of the photograph, using the pierced holes as a guide, position the steel ruler, and with an X-acto knife, trim away the excess edges of the photograph, leaving just the portion seen in the outlined window.

For the other shapes (when purchased plastic templates are not available in the desired size or shape), use the same basic method to make your photo cropper. Draw around cookie cutters, glass rims, or other objects to mark the acetate or plastic bag. Or trace a shape from the patterns on pages 200–221 onto tracing paper or use a photocopy of a pattern. (See page 50 for how to enlarge or reduce sizes on a photocopier.) And, of course, you can draw your own shapes. Slip the tracing, photocopy, or drawing under the acetate or plastic bag and mark the outline with a ballpoint pen (use a steel ruler to help draw any straight lines). When you have made your shaped window on the acetate, carefully cut out the tracing, photocopy, or drawing of the shape to use later as a cutting guide.

Position the acetate window over the photograph as you want to cut it. Prick the outline with a pin at several key points, then remove the acetate. Flip the photograph over, and matching the pierced marks to the cutout shape (reversing the cutout shape as well by flipping it over), very lightly draw the shape onto the back of the photograph and cut it out using an X-acto knife.

How to Use Color Photocopying

By using a color photocopier, a whole new range of options arises for the innovative scrapbooker. You can make color photocopies of your photographs to use in your album—a good idea if you wish to crop your pictures or silhouette them. You can also make copies of the clip art and reproduce the line art provided at the back of this book, printing it in colored inks or coloring it in yourself afterwards. Fabric and three-dimensional objects—everything from candy to small souvenirs to flowers—can also be reproduced and used (over and over again if you wish) on your album pages.

While there are often times that we feel like sharing our memories and creative efforts with family and friends across the nation and perhaps around the globe, the effort and expense that would go into producing a duplicate copy of a scrapbook can be daunting, and in the case of an heirloom album virtually impossible. Luckily, modern color photocopying technology is such that identical pages can be reproduced with very little effort. Entire albums can be created for members of the family who were unable to attend a special function (such as a reunion or a wedding anniversary celebration, for instance) or a diligently collected reconstruction of a family tree can be sent to all of its distant branches.

Before you begin, it pays to research the color quality, prices, and store policies of a number of different photocopying outlets before you entrust one with your special project. Ask what kind of copier is being used (laser is preferred), and request a few samples. Once you've made the commitment, some shops will run off test copies until you're pleased with the results—no extra charge. Whether the tests are free or need to be paid for, it is crucial that they be done, considering the fact that a slightly off-color reproduction can mar the hard-earned effect of your pages. Make a friend of the copy-shop person who will be working with you; that way he's more likely to understand your needs and will give you the best quality reproduction possible.

No matter what method of color photocopying you choose, it helps to be familiar with copyright laws. According to the US Copyright Act, an artist has the right "to prevent any intentional distortion, mutilation, or other modification" of his or her work. That includes photocopying, for no one ever really knows what the end result of the photocopying will be. Unless the artist has granted you written permission to copy his work, the only art you can legally reproduce is that which is considered part of the public domain. Clip art, like that included in the back of this book, is perfectly legal to reproduce for your own use and as gifts. In fact, we encourage you to do so. Just remember, reselling things you have made with clip art is not allowed.

It's a given that color photocopies will not last as long as the photographs themselves, but if they are produced patiently on a high-quality copier and stored with the same care as you would give to any original photograph, they should be around to give pleasure for years to come. The copies should be deacidified, mounted on buffered, pH-neutral album pages, and surrounded by archival-quality polyester sleeves before being placed in a scrapbook. And this new album, as with all important scrapbooks, photographs, and documents, should be kept away from the damaging effects of light and humidity.

How to Include Journal Entries and Titles

While a picture may be worth a thousand words, words are still useful to enhance the significance of your photographs and to tell your special story. You can use them to inscribe or dedicate a book to someone as a gift.

Simple titles, names of people, or place names can identify the photographs for the viewer. You can cut names from travel brochures, postcards, or magazines. Even other comments ("wow," "star," "fantastic," "powerhouse," etc.) can add spark or humor to the pages—check advertisements and sports pages for colorful words. You can write your own titles with cut-out or stenciled letters or write on a small rectangle of paper; mount the rectangle on contrasting-colored paper or add a small vertical strip to transform it into a signpost.

Longer descriptions can add much interesting information about places and people shown in your book and are useful in travel books or to note special or unusual happenings. It is a good idea to keep the descriptions interesting, relevant, and short—about a paragraph per page—to retain the visual impact of the book. If you find you have a great deal of information to share, as with a travelogue or a complete journal, you may want to make a separate companion volume to go with your picture album.

Your comments should be easy to read. To generate your text, use a computer printer, a typewriter, or, if your write by hand, use your best printing, penmanship, or calligraphy, to turn your comments into an artful part of the page.

The text can be written in a block, within a special shaped outline, or as line captions under several photographs. If you wish, mount the comment paper onto contrasting-colored paper, or frame and decorate it to fit the page decor.

MAKING YOUR SCRAPBOOK

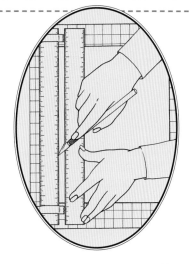

Although there are many styles of scrapbooks, notebooks, and albums for sale, you may still want to create a special, one-of-a-kind book of your own design. Although our books are easy to make and require no special skills or unusual supplies, they can be decorated as lavishly or as simply as you wish. Once you have learned how to make one of our books, you will be able to design a book of your own in any size or shape.

THE BASIC BOOK

1. From foam core or mat board, cut two covers the desired size for your album, making sure they are exactly the same size (page 50). To make the spine of the album, cut two strips of card stock, each the same length as the album cover and 2 inches wide. (This allows for a ½-inch-thick spine to accommodate the album

pages; allow extra if you are using foam core for

THE BASIC BOOK AND THE TRADITIONAL BOOK

YOU WILL NEED:

* Foam core or mat board for covers
* Card stock or heavy bond paper for spine
* Acid-free glue
* Brush to apply glue
* Spray adhesive
* X-acto knife
* Steel ruler
* Pencil
* Album pages
* Paper or fabric for cover and inside-cover liner
* Decorative cord, ⅛" diameter

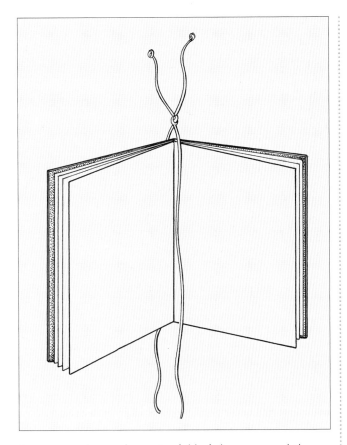

Lay one cord over the center fold of the pages and the other cord under the spine, as shown.

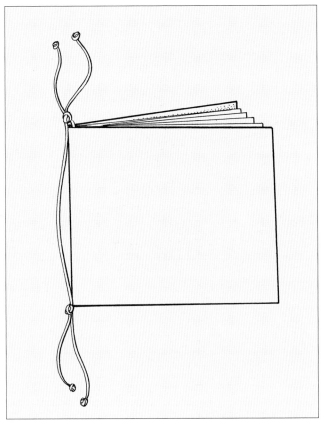

Knot cord ends just below the spine to hold pages to the album.

THE TRADITIONAL BOOK

1. From foam core or mat board, cut two covers exactly the same size (page 50). We suggest a cover size 9" x 11½" or slightly larger, since this size will easily accommodate standard-size paper (8½" x 11") for album pages. Cut a 1½-inch strip off one edge of each cover for a binding strip.

2. Centered on one binding strip, and mark the position for six holes, spaced evenly, with the first hole about 1¼ inches from the top edge and the last hole about 1¼ inches above the bottom edge. Carefully punch a hole at each mark with an awl, or a single-hole paper punch, or cut a tiny ✗ with an X-acto knife. Make corresponding holes on the other binding strip.

3. Cut two hinge strips, each about 1¾ inches wide by 9 inches (or the height of your book). With a brush, apply acid-free glue to the

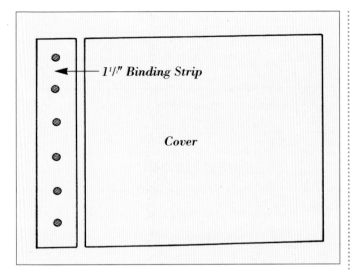

Mark and punch six holes on each binding strip.

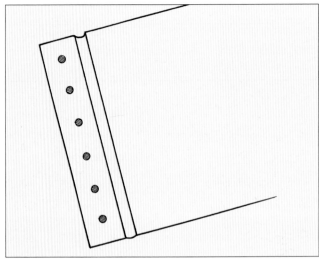

Glue hinge strip to underside of binding strip and cover, leaving ¼" space between.

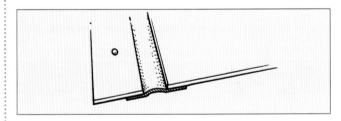

Close-up of hinge strip glued in place.

edges of one hinge strip (leaving the center ¼ inch free of glue), and adhere the hinge to the underside of the front cover and its binding strip, leaving a ¼-inch space between the two boards to form the hinge. Repeat for the back cover.

4. Cover and line the front and back boards with fabric or paper (see Steps 2 and 3 of the Basic Book, page 70). Directly over the binding strip holes, cut holes in cover paper or fabric, using an X-acto knife to make tiny ✗'s.

5. Use standard-size, acid-free stationery paper for your album pages, or cut your own from other acid-free paper. With a single-hole paper punch, punch holes along one edge of the pages to correspond to the cover holes. Place the pages inside the album cover, matching the holes. Make spacer strips (page 55) if desired.

6. Cut two 24-inch lengths of decorative cord. Use a yarn needle or wrap tape tightly around one end of the cord to make threading easier. Starting at the front top hole, thread one cord down through the front hole, all the pages, the back, then thread it back up to the front through the next hole, then continue weaving it in and out down to the bottom hole. In the same manner, thread the other cord through the holes from bottom to top as shown on page 74.

Bring the ends of each cord to the front at top and bottom and tie into bows. Trim the cord ends and knot to prevent unraveling.

A,B,C = *scrapbook width plus ¼ inch for ease (for spiral-bound scrapbooks, do not include the spiral coil in the width measurement, and omit the added ¼ inch)*

D,E = *scrapbook length plus ¼ inch*

F = *total scrapbook depth plus ¼ inch*

G = *total scrapbook depth plus ⅜ inch (the same as F plus ⅛ inch)*

On the diagram, solid lines indicate cutting lines; broken lines (B and E) are fold lines.

3. Using an X-acto knife and a steel ruler, cut out the slipcase. Score, but do not cut through, the board along each fold line (the unscored surface will be the inside of the slipcase). Cut a small notch ½ inch deep at the center of each D edge, as indicated (omit for spiral-bound album).

4. To assemble the slipcase, carefully fold the sides away from the spine at right angles; fold the top and bottom flaps to meet the edge of the opposite side. Tape the flap edges (C) to the side edges (A).

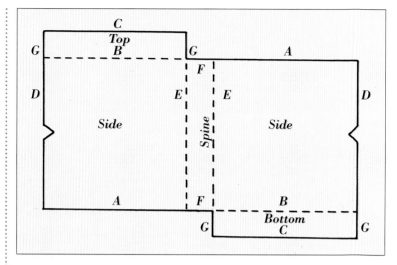

Pattern for Slipcase. Solid lines are cutting lines; broken lines are fold lines.

5. If desired, cover the slipcase with paper or fabric, using spray adhesive.

Note: You can also buy special archival boxes or use another box, covering and lining it with acid-free paper, to store your scrapbook.

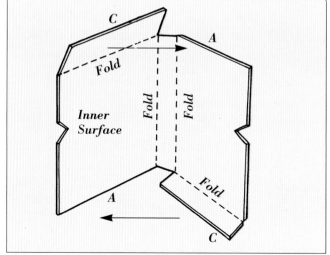

Fold top and bottom edges so C meets A to form slipcase.

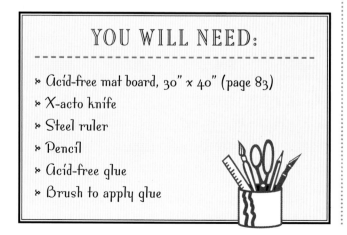

YOU WILL NEED:

- Acid-free mat board, 30" x 40" (page 83)
- X-acto knife
- Steel ruler
- Pencil
- Acid-free glue
- Brush to apply glue

MAKING A COLLAGE

BASIC STEPS

Here we show a page from one of our books to demonstrate the simple, basic process of creating a collage. You can adapt the techniques to fit your own special materials.

Begin by arranging your photographs on your memory-book page, then embellishing them with the prepared collage material (page 86). Use removable tape to hold all the layered pieces together and to keep the collage in place. If you want to lift the pieces to rearrange them, you will find the tape is easy to handle and reuse. To ensure that your final placement will be glued exactly as you have arranged it, lightly pencil-mark the position of each piece, starting with the top layer and ending with the bottom layer. The pencil marks can be removed with a kneaded eraser after gluing.

Use removable tape and a light pencil to mark the position of the pieces for the collage.

> **"I'll note you in my book of memory."**
>
> —William Shakespeare

MEMORY BOUQUETS

Just as you might pick a glorious bunch of springtime blooms, gathering the most distinctive, the most colorful, and the most festive flowers from the bounty of your personal garden, you can also collect powerful and beautiful memories from life to create another kind of bouquet—a heartfelt arrangement of your most evocative objects of remembrance. Whether it is to be enjoyed by a loved one or is just for yourself, a scrapbook gives deep pleasure to those fortunate enough to wander through its pages—particularly when they are the subject of the story. And the scrapbook has a special glory if prepared in proper archival fashion, which is distinct from your garden: It will never fade. A scrapbook will continue to be a source of joy long after the last garden bloom has fallen.

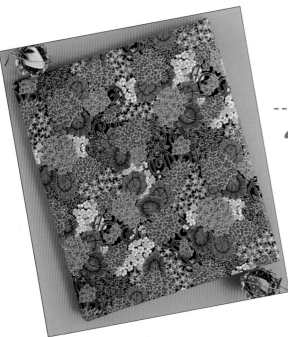

A GARDEN FOR MOTHER

Picture a leisurely stroll through an abundant garden and imagine being able to transform this experience into a floral scrapbook that you could give to a loved one. Bursting with flowers and photographs of family and friends, this paradise on paper is designed to delight the horticulture lover—be it a mother or a good friend. Using reproductions of engravings from Victorian seed catalogues, glorious floral fabrics, colorful art clipped from printed pictures, and a lovely floral alphabet, you, too, can create a scrapbook that is a veritable garden for all seasons.

COVERED WITH LOVE

▲ Cover the album (page 52) with fabric.

• For pages, you'll need to keep fabric edges from fraying and make the fabric stiff enough to cut with the decorative paper edgers (which won't cut untreated fabric). Use a strong-bonding fusible web fabric to bond the fabric to lightweight acid-free paper following the manufacturer's directions.

A PORTRAIT AMONG THE FLOWERS

▶ This portrait is decorated with enlarged photocopies (page 50) of clip-art flowers and letters (page 182) that spell out a special name.

• The photocopies are colored with pencils or markers, then cut out with cuticle scissors.

• The picture is mounted under a rectangle of fabric cut with a decorative edge using paper edgers (page 57). If your floral pattern is suitable, you could also cut a wandering edge that follows the shape of the floral design.

• One or more graduated layers of coordinated colors are added as a border.

MOTHER IN BLOOM

▲ The young gardener is pictured tending her most precious flower, her child. The two are shown together with a photograph of morning glories and enlarged (page 50) clip-art flowers.

• Throughout the book, clip-art motifs are used—enlarged and reduced as desired for a familiar yet varied look.

FRAMED IN PARADISE

▲ This portrait is framed by a page-sized field of flowered fabric with wandering edges.

• The fabric is cut with cuticle scissors and the shape of the floral pattern is followed to overlap, but not obscure, the subject of the picture. A small, closely patterned fabric works especially well here because it allows for decorative shaping that still follows the photograph's edge fairly closely.

YOU WILL NEED:

❧ Basic supplies (page 42)

<u>Supplies for this scrapbook:</u>

❧ Traditional store-bought album

❧ Fabric for cover

❧ Coordinating decorative floral prints

❧ Colored papers

❧ Fusible web

❧ Lightweight acid-free white paper

❧ Paper crimper

❧ Clip-art (page 182)

> **"For memory has painted this**
>
> **perfect day**
>
> **With colors that never fade..."**
>
> —CARRIE JACOBS BOND

A FLORAL SILHOUETTE

◆

◄ Decorate a spread with a burst of thematic illustrative art, including old or new printed pictures of favorite flowers (seed catalogues are an easy source).

• To create the flower silhouettes, cut out flowers by cutting away the background with cuticle scissors.

• Be sure to deacidify all paper clippings (page 46), unless you are certain they are acid-free.

• Enlarge photocopies of the clip-art, coloring the copies as you wish.

CRIMPED FRAME

◆

◄ For the bright red frame, crimp the paper by drawing it lengthwise through a crimper (page 48) to form vertical ridges.

• Cut the frame edges with decorative paper edgers (page 57).

• Continue the arrangement of the cut-out flowers, as on the facing page, overlapping the photograph and frame.

Our clip-art roses (page 183) can be added to the other floral illustrations.

A GIANT FLOWER FRAME

·············◆·············

▶ A grand, enlarged flower makes a fascinating frame for the small photograph. You can cut out the flower center to make a frame or you can crop the photograph (page 65) or photocopy it (page 67) so that it fits over the flower center.

• The oversized watering can is enlarged from the clip art (page 223). Color the flower and the watering can with colored pencils or markers.

• Use a large piece of fabric as a backdrop for the page.

FLORAL FRAMES

·············◆·············

▶ Frame the two photographs with a narrow border of floral fabric mounted on paper and cut along the edges with decorative paper edgers.

• Make a page-sized frame of floral fabric and place it over a colored inner frame (with a smaller picture opening). Cut both layers with decorative edges.

Decorating with Fabric

We used actual fabric for this album, but color photocopies can also be used for background, strips, and cutouts.

THROUGH THE YEARS

This scrapbook is a tribute to an extraordinary woman; it is a record of her life, of everything and everyone she has treasured. In fact, the fabric used on the album's cover is an actual piece of curtain from her grandmother's home. The same fabric has been color-photocopied and used as both backdrop and as an element in a recurring motif on the book's inside pages. Here, Lee, the subject of the book, is seen at the age of seven, on through her blushing teens, to a robust and healthy fifty. The technique of interspersing old photographs and memorabilia with current images collapses time so that one has the feeling that past and future can exist simultaneously. And with the help of a well-thought-out scrapbook, it can. This is a wonderful example of how you can design with pictures from the past, even taking an entire page from an old album and giving it a fresh look through inventive layouts and vibrant color.

A LIVING COVER

▲ Before gluing fabric onto the album cover, see page 67 regarding photo-copying fabric. Cover the album with a piece of antique fabric (page 52).

BLENDING OLD AND NEW

▶ The simple antique oval mat frames an up-to-date picture of the person whose history this book portrays.

• The double-colored outline on the mat is drawn with the same colors shown in the photograph, to unite old and new.

Lee Monaco
Her Life in Pictures

A SPECIAL GRANDMOTHER

*a*n invaluable cache of turn-of-the-century photographs serves as the starting point for this festive scrapbook, influencing every design element, from the nostalgic floral fabric on the album's cover to the turn-of-the-century images of butterflies and flowers and the color choices on the inside pages. The fragile nature of the photographs, and the fact that they had been previously mounted on cardboard, both affected the look of the final pages. A message of love to a special grandmother about her long and fruitful life, this unusual scrapbook proves that you can take an assortment of photographs that seem dated and refashion them with a modern look.

A COVER BLOOM

▲ Cover the outside of the notebook with fabric (page 52).

• Cut a length of ribbon 2 inches longer than the cover. With spray adhesive, mount it onto the fabric cover, wrapping the ends over the edge to the inside of the cover.

• Cut the inner (end) sheets for the cover (page 54) and adhere them to the inside cover, overlapping the cover flaps and the ribbon ends. Decorate the inner sheets with color photocopies (page 67) of the clip-art (page 182).

• Brush a generous coat of acid-free

glue onto the back of the sunflower and attach it to the cover. Hold it in place with T-pins while the glue dries.

• Cut out the butterfly, and with spray adhesive, mount it onto bristol board or card stock. Cut out the shape. Adhere a foam disk under each wing; mount onto the sunflower.

IN HER GARDEN

▲ Flower-fresh shades of pink border the photograph, with clip-art flowers at each corner.

• Make color photocopies of the clip-art you want to use and cut them out with small scissors.

YOU WILL NEED:

❧ Basic Supplies (page 42)

Supplies for this scrapbook:

❧ Three-ring notebook binder
❧ Fabric for cover
❧ Clip-art (page 182)
❧ Paper for liners
❧ Fabric sunflower
❧ T-pins
❧ White acid-free bristol board or card stock for album pages
❧ Acid-free paper (store-bought or handmade paper) in assorted colors
❧ Ribbons in various widths
❧ Paper lace doilies
❧ Gift tags

GEORGE AND MABEL

............◆............

▶ This portrait is nicely set off on the page with richly layered royal blue shaded mountings. Note that the corners of the colored rectangles are rounded.

• Trim decorative corners with a corner paper punch (page 60), or simply round them off with scissors. Add clip-art as desired.

Copying Old Photos

The heirloom photographs can be reproduced on a color copier set on the black-and-white mode. See page 67 for more information on color copying.

LACED WITH HISTORY

............◆............

◀ Ribbons and a lace doily—together with the clip-art trims— give this page an old-fashioned, feminine charm. For more complete directions on how to assemble this page, see "Making a Collage" on page 85, where this page serves as the example.

Rubber stamps for our clip-art images are also available from Rubber Stampede (page 48).

"Great is the human who has not lost his childlike heart."

MENG TSE (4TH CENTURY B.C.)

GREAT MILESTONES

These are the momentous and memorable occasions that form the very foundations of our lives—weddings, births, bar mitzvahs, christenings. They define who we are, where we come from, and where we are going. And often, despite their great importance, we are so busy with the festivities at hand while these events are taking place that precious minutes, hours, even days can pass by in a convivial blur. This is why such occasions have traditionally been the stuff of scrapbooks; for the last century at least, wedding albums and baby books have been instrumental in recording these joyous moments. Yet today's version of the traditional scrapbook or photo album can be a far cry from the one you may have grown up with.

THE WEDDING BOOK

*G*country wedding—what better way to celebrate the nature of love and respect for the natural world? While creating a scrapbook to commemorate a wedding is a time-honored custom, this updated version, which features a palette of earth-inspired colors and a wealth of natural materials, evokes both a sense of tradition and a forward-looking respect for the environment. The store-bought album is re-covered in earth-friendly, kraft-type paper and embellished with decorative rubber stamps in a soft green flower motif. The inside pages continue the flower theme with a combination of stamps, punched paper details, and ribbon leaves, with gold embossing for a touch of dew-like sparkle. Printed memorabilia produced for the wedding complement the wide range of candid photographs, creating a casual ambience.

A COVER OF ROSES

▲ Disassemble the store-bought scrapbook. Measure and cut the paper for the front and back covers (see page 52).

• Following "How to Stamp a Double-imprint Design" on page 64, stamp the cover with scattered roses, first with the ivory paint, then with the green paint, to create a shadow effect. Let the paint dry completely.

• Using spray adhesive, cover the front and back covers. Cut the paper for the liners and mount on the inside of each cover.

YOU WILL NEED:

* Basic supplies (page 42)
Supplies for this scrapbook:
* Post-style scrapbook
* White acid-free paper for album pages
* Foam core board or mat board for spacer strips
* Paper for cover and liner
* Stamping paint in two colors (we used ivory and green)
* Fine-textured foam sponge for paint application
* Foam-surfaced design stamps with large designs of a rose, a heart, and a fleur-de-lis, the letters L, O, V, E, and a small design of a fleur-de-lis
* Printed paper ribbon
* Green leaves-by-the-yard trim
* Wide green ribbon
* Gold and green decorative ribbon
* Decorative craft paper punch with fleur-de-lis design
* Acid-free paper (store-bought or handmade) in green, tan, and ivory
* Wedding memorabilia

Wedding photography courtesy of Casual Candids Washington Crossing, Pennsylvania.

A DISTINCTIVE INSIDE COVER

▲ Cut three different-colored squares of paper and graduate the sizes 1/4-inch all around. Stamp a double imprint of the large fleur-de-lis on the center of the smallest square. Center the squares and glue them together. Cut a duplicate set of squares; double-imprint a rose on the small square. Glue the sets together.

• Center one set of squares and glue to the inside of the front cover (on the liner), using acid-free glue; glue the other set to the inside back cover.

• Cut 4 leaves from the leaves-by-the-yard trim. Glue one to each corner. Repeat on the back.

• If you are using your own album pages, see page 54.

• Cut spacer strips the length and width of the binder strips (page 55), making as many as needed to separate the pages of your album, and allowing room for added materials.

INVITATION TO LOVE

▲ Cut a tan rectangle, and an ivory rectangle 1/4-inch smaller .

• Lightly pencil-mark the position for stamping L O V E onto the ivory paper. Stamp a single imprint (page 64) over each pencil mark.

• Cut a photograph or a colored photocopy to fit the opening of the letter O (not shown here). To make a mat as a photo cropper (page 66), stamp an O on a rectangle of scrap paper and cut out the center. Use leaf trim to frame the L O V E paper.

• Deacidify the envelope and invitation, unless you are certain that the paper is acid free (page 14).

• Using the decorative paper punch (page 59), punch one fleur-de-lis each from tan-and-green paper. Cut a square to back each shape.

• Cut a rectangle of green paper 1/8 -inch larger all around than the invitation.

• With green paint, stamp a small fleur-de-lis on a separate piece of ivory paper. Let dry, and cut out the shape.

• Crop the wedding-ring photograph (page 65).

• Make a paper ribbon bow. Cut separate leaves from leaf trim.

• Attach paper pieces following the photograph and "Making a Collage" on page 85.

HEARTS AND FLOWERS

·············◆·············

▼ Cut two lengths each of wide green ribbon and green-and-gold ribbon to fit across the page. Cut a notch at each end.

• From green paper, cut a rectangle 1/4-inch larger all around than your large photograph.

• Stamp double imprints (page 64) of two roses and one heart, using ivory and green paint on tan paper. Let dry and cut out.

• Cut out the center of the stamped heart to frame the photograph.

• For each of the two photographs, cut a green rectangle 1/8 inch larger than the pictures.

• Arrange and attach the pieces following the photograph and " Making a Collage" (page 85).

THE KISS

·············◆·············

▼ Cut a green and a tan rectangle, each 1 3/8 inches larger than the photograph. On the tan paper, cut away a 1 3/8-inch square at each corner, leaving a center border strip at each edge that matches the width and length of the photograph.

• Using the decorative paper punch (page 59), punch out fleurs-de-lis along the tan borders.

• Using green paint, stamp four large fleurs-de-lis on ivory pape. Cut out the shapes. Assemble frame as shown

• Using the decorative paper punch, punch out six fleurs-de-lis across the top and bottom edges of the album page. Cut two 1 1/2-inch-wide strips of tan paper to fit across the page and on the reverse side; glue strips to underline the cutouts.

• Cut a green paper rectangle 1/8-inch larger than the name card. Decorate with leaves from trim.

Wedding Moments

Cherished paper mementos from the wedding can be used on these pages.

HEART OF HEARTS

A heart of birch and handmade papyrus pages make this small but lovely scrapbook a unique treasure. The use of natural materials makes the traditional shape seem refreshingly contemporary. This sincere, unadorned album gives tribute to those you love, or would be a great gift for all the members of the wedding party.

HEART COVER

▶ Enlarge the pattern (page 50) for the heart shape on page 221. Following the directions for the "Wood Books" on page 78, make the heart-shaped cover, cutting out the small heart on the front and making shaped album pages (page 54) to fit. A natural finish is shown, but the wood can be easily painted and trimmed with details as well.

▶ You can make a heart-shaped photo cropper (page 66) to crop the photographs or color photocopies to fit the heart-shaped pages. Mount the photographs onto the pages with photo-mount squares.

YOU WILL NEED:

- ❧ Basic supplies (page 42)

Supplies for this scrapbook:

- ❧ 1/4" birch plywood
- ❧ 2 large notebook rings
- ❧ Papyrus for album pages
- ❧ Clear polyurethane spray or primer and cover paint
- ❧ Deacidification spray (for papyrus)

READY FOR HIS CLOSE-UPS

▲▶ Crop photographs or photocopies (page 65) to 2 3/8-inch squares. For each photograph, cut the largest paper square (for the bottom layer) to measure 4 3/4 inches square.

• Cut layers of squares, diamonds, or circles in assorted baby colors, making them smaller as you work toward the top. Cut straight edges or decorative edges, regular corners or shaped ones, and punch through one or more layers, as you please.

• Mount the photographs on the top layer, adding punched-out stars and hearts if desired.

• Arrange the decorated photographs across the pages, adding a rectangle, decorated at the edges, for journal entries, including the baby's name, birthdate, weight, stories, first books, and amusing first words and sentences.

▲ Decorative cut edges with punched-out hearts frame the photograph while a woven ribbon and added hearts trim the border.

MY PARENTS

▼ Make paper corner mounts (page 61) to hold the photograph in place.

• Add punched-out shapes or clip-art as desired.

Saving Punchouts

Don't toss those punched-out shapes; they can be used later as page decorations.

• The simple treatment of the single photograph of the baby's parents provides visual contrast to the elaborate baby pages.

WRAPPED IN RIBBONS

▼ The photograph of the baby is held in place by diagonal cuts in the album page. The picture itself is framed with fancy punched corners and narrow strips cut with decorative paper edgers that transform the rectangular photograph into a dynamic diamond-shaped center for the page.

• Ribbons and more strips fill out the corners, which are finished off with more decoratively punched corners.

> ❝The most important thing parents can teach their children is how to get along without them.❞
>
> —FRANK A. CLARK

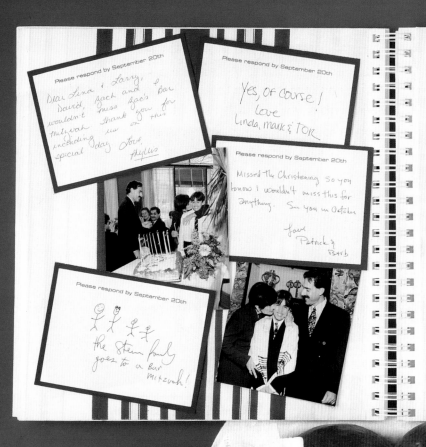

'Tis a Gift to Be Simple

If you wish, make a scrapbook of a christening, first communion, or confirmation using simple, dignified trims, as we did in this album, in keeping with the religious theme.

A SHARED CEREMONY

················◆················

▲ The photographs of the celebration are the focus of this collage composed of RSVP notes and photographs of the service, all underlined by the vertically striped shawl.

• The RSVP notes are each mounted on royal-blue paper with a narrow border.

• The four photos of family and friends participating in the ceremonies are arranged simply and closely, mounted on a large rectangle of royal blue. The center of the page is embellished with a 2 3/4-inch-wide Star of David with points and center cut out, and backed with a slightly larger silver star.

EMILY'S SWEET SIXTEEN

Often a tender, poignant story is best expressed with a few carefully selected words. This purchased, handmade scrapbook tells the story of a special girl as she grows from a baby to a beautiful teen—not with a million snapshots but with several selective but wholly revealing images that reflect her essential nature. Here is Emily as a baby, holding her baby brother, with a dear friend, and trying on makeup and looking glamorous. With the telling simplicity of a Haiku, these photographs (all taken by her father) offer brief, gemlike moments. Handmade, flower-embedded paper and brief, calligraphic captions further enhance the delicate nature of this book and its subject, making it a wonderful sweet sixteen or graduation gift.

COVERED IN FLOWERS

▶ Buy a similar album or make a laced scrapbook (page 74), covering it with flower-embedded rice paper. Alternatively, you can decorate a plain piece of rice paper with pressed-flower stickers (see next page). However, unprotected dried flowers that are not embedded in the paper (as our cover bouquet was) will be too fragile to use on the cover.

• Make a tightly braided cord with three strands of raffia. This will be the final tie cord used to assemble the cover and pages.

A SENSE OF SOLITUDE

............◆............

▲ On these pages only one photograph is used. The left page displays a horizontal rectangle of handmade paper with embedded flowers and calligraphy to complement the photograph on the right, which is mounted on a large piece of handmade paper and edged with several flower stickers.

Practicing on Plain Paper

- -

To prevent damage to delicate handmade paper, practice calligraphic word arrangements on a piece of plain scrap paper the size of your page. Then cut out the shape the words create and experiment with incorporating that shape into the final page layouts. When you're satisfied with the words' position for each page layout, add them directly to the pages or create special additional paper shapes that are then glued in place.

FIFTY LOVING YEARS

This scrapbook really commemorates two events: the wedding, fifty years ago, of a couple deeply in love, and the celebration, fifty years later, of that same couple, still as enamored of each other as when they first said "I do." The scrapbook combines photographs from the original wedding party with those from the current festivities; the original wedding invitation; and images of all the family members, children, and grandchildren who attended the fifty-years bash. And because it has been created with archival materials, this album will—like true love—stand the test of time.

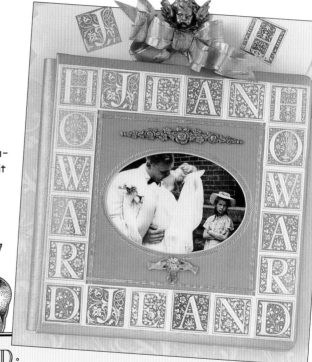

KISSING COVER

▶ Cover album with gold paper. Plan spacing for the letter border, spelling out one name along the sides and the other across the top and bottom. If the names are very short, consider using last initials or blank or embellished squares to fill the spaces. (For our 6" x 6" square border, we cut the initial note cards to 1 7/8-inch squares.)

• Cut the outer edge of the purchased mat to fit the inner edge of the planned border.

• Cut strips of gold-foil ribbon to fit the inner edge of the letter border.

• Arrange the pieces following the photograph and "Making a Collage" on page 85. Glue the paper in place on a 12-inch square of acid-free paper with acid-free glue.

• Glue on the desired embellishments, and glue the collage unit to the front cover, with a protective sleeve covering it.

YOU WILL NEED:

* Basic supplies (page 42)

Supplies for this scrapbook:
* Scrapbook
* Album pages to fit
* Clear plastic sleeves to fit album pages
* Mat with gold trim
* Gold initial note cards with the letters needed to spell the couple's first names, LOVE, and FAMILY and clip-art initials (page 199)

* Acid-free white paper (store-bought or handmade)
* Imprintable mats to fit photographs, color-photocopied in a gold tone
* Vellum (heavyweight tracing paper)
* Sturdy gold-foil paper
* Embossed and textured gold papers
* Gold paper with printed design
* Narrow gold-foil ribbon or tape
* Small gold embellishments

* Metallic gold marker
* Black fine-point marker
* Decorative paper edgers with two different patterns
* Decorative craft paper punches with heart and corner designs
* Store-bought plastic template for decorative border

THE LOVING COUPLE

▶ Trim the edges of the large photograph or colored photocopy with the decorative paper edger.

• Cut a piece of gold paper $1/2$ inch larger all around than the photograph, using different paper edgers.

• Using the edgers, cut out $2 1/2$-inch squares from the initial note cards for L O V E and $2 3/4$-inch squares for the couple's first initials. Use the gold marker to draw a $1/4$-inch border all around the larger squares.

• Deacidify the name tag.

• Arrange the pieces, following the photograph and "Making a Collage" on page 85, adding a gold cupid and a heart embellishment.

THE WHOLE GANG

▶ Cut a $9 1/2$-inch rectangle from gold paper, cutting the short edges with a paper edger. Cut a gold-foil rectangle 1 inch larger all around than the photograph.

• Cut a white rectangle $3/8$-inch smaller than the gold piece for a frame. Centered on the white paper, measure, mark, and cut an opening to fit the photograph. Cut a $3 1/4$-inch square of white paper. Working freehand, lightly pencil-draw a family tree or crest design; use the gold marker to color it (or use the black marker and color-copy in a gold tone). Cut four strips of gold-foil paper to fit the sides of the drawing.

• Attach the pieces following the photograph and "Making a Collage," adding a gold cupid embellishment.

FAMILY

"God gave us memories
so that we may
have roses in December."
—JAMES M. BARRIE

> "Nothing great
> was ever achieved without
> enthusiasm."
> —RALPH WALDO EMERSON

JUST FOR JOY

Scrapbooking today has expanded beyond the documentation of a family's history or a child's growth. It has become a marvelous expression of the pleasures of everyday life. A boy's Little League game, a day on rollerblades, a few days in the life of a young brother and sister—all provide rich material for albums that remind us that it is the small events and routines of our lives that bring us the most joy. The playful nature of these albums attests to that spirit. In this section many of the scrapbooks are made from foam core board, which is a terrific material for countless album ideas.

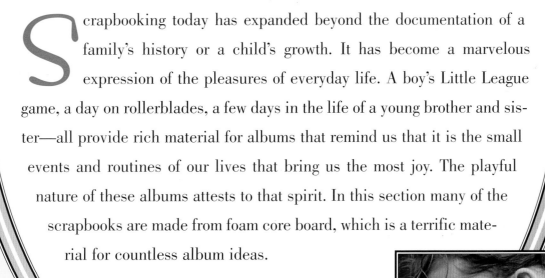

THE SOCCER BOOK

The spirit of competition and the excitement of team sports are captured in this easy-to-make foam core board album cut in the shape of a soccer ball. You might want to commemorate a young soccer player's most important game or perhaps design a tribute to his or her entire team and represent friendships that may stand the test of time. The individual facets of the soccer ball itself provide an interesting design element and an opportunity to insert cropped photographs of faces, action shots, trophies, and winning goals. It's a wonderful tribute to a child's pleasure in athletics.

the soccer ball, as shown on page 215. Trace the pattern onto white paper. Using an X-acto knife, carefully cut out the black sections. (Retain the enlarged pattern to use later as you decorate the album pages.) Using spray adhesive, center the white piece and attach it to the black paper cover.

PLAY HARD!

◄ Trace the enlarged pattern onto black paper and cut out the black pieces to use as overlying pieces.

• To make a pattern for cropping the photographs, start by using the enlarged pattern to trace one of the white hexagonal sections onto scrap paper. Then adjust the pattern so that the inner line matches the edge of the center pentagon, the outer edges match the curve of the album page, and the adjoining side edges are at the center of the black dividing line. Cut out the pattern.

• Check that the pattern will fit accurately around the center black pentagon with the adjoining sides butting.

COVER THE NET

▲ Following the special directions for using foam core board under "Foam Board Books," page 80, cut two 10-inch-diameter circles from the foam core board and make holes for two rings.

• Cut the album pages (see page

54), using half black paper and half white. Alternate colors as you assemble the book.

• Cut a square of black paper larger than the cover board. Using spray adhesive, attach the paper to the cover. Trim away the excess paper.

• Enlarge the pattern (page 50) for

- Use the pattern to make a photo cropper (page 66).

- Select and crop five photographs to fit into the window.

- Arrange the cropped pictures and the center black pentagon on the album page. Glue the pentagon in place with acid-free glue and use photo-mount squares to attach the photographs. Following the enlarged pattern for placement, attach the black-paper overlying pieces. Trim away any excess paper.

GREAT FRAME BALLS

..............◆..............

▶ Using a photocopier, make eight copies of the printed soccer ball, reducing the size to make one 4½ inches across, two each 4 inches across, two each 2½ inches across, and the remaining three graduated from 1¼ inches to 2 inches across. Cut out the shapes.

- Cut the black pentagon from the center of each of the five largest balls to make frames.

- Select the photographs to fit the windows. Trim away any excess edges on the photographs.

YOU WILL NEED:

- -

❋ Basic supplies (page 42)

Supplies for this scrapbook:

❋ Foam core board, 1/8" or 3/16" thick

❋ Large notebook rings

❋ Acid-free black and white paper for album pages

❋ Decorative single-hole paper punch

❋ White pencil or markers

- Attach the pieces to a black page, following the photograph and "Making a Collage" on page 85.

THE KICK

..............◆..............

▶ Using the enlarged soccer-ball pattern, make a white cutout section as you did for the cover.

- Center the white piece over a black album page and pencil-mark the position of the edges for the center pentagon opening. Remove the white piece. Position the photograph over the marked pentagon, so that the subject is centered and the edges of the picture cover the marked edge. Attach the photograph with photo-mount squares.

- Using spray adhesive, attach the white paper to the page with the pentagon opening framing the photograph. Trim away any excess paper.

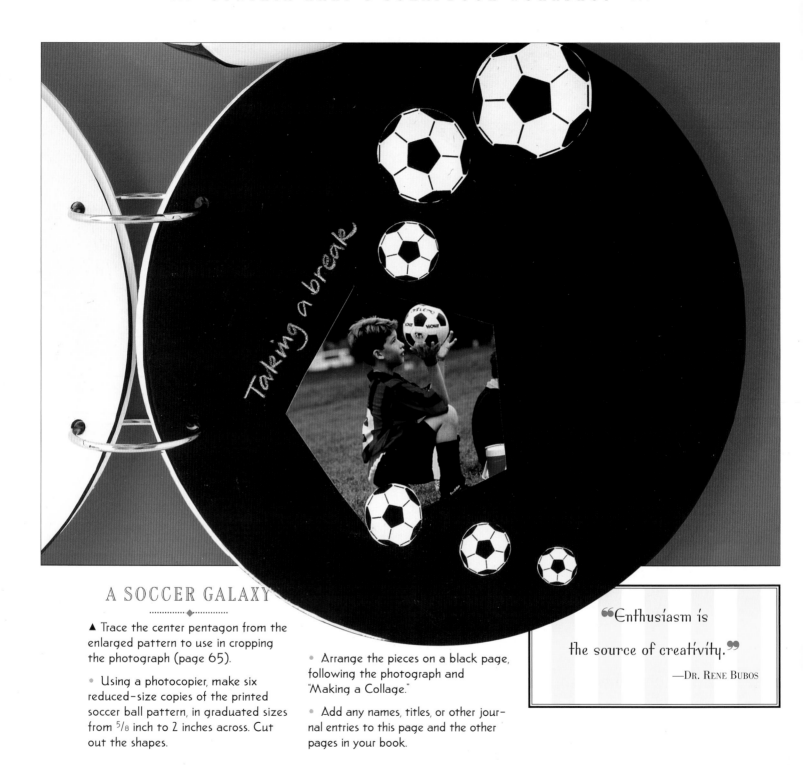

Taking a break

A SOCCER GALAXY

▲ Trace the center pentagon from the enlarged pattern to use in cropping the photograph (page 65).

• Using a photocopier, make six reduced-size copies of the printed soccer ball pattern, in graduated sizes from ⁵/₈ inch to 2 inches across. Cut out the shapes.

• Arrange the pieces on a black page, following the photograph and "Making a Collage."

• Add any names, titles, or other journal entries to this page and the other pages in your book.

> ❝Enthusiasm is the source of creativity.❞
>
> —DR. RENE BUBOS

THE HAPPY FACE BOOK

This sunny, smiley-faced scrapbook cele-brates the precious moments shared by a dynamic brother-and-sister duo as they delight in childhood. Here are a few of their favorite things: her first dance recital, his first ride in the cab of a semi-truck, a flawless day on the seashore. A variety of brightly colored candy, which has been arranged in page lay-outs, then photocopied and used for everything from lettering to embellishments, adds an inventive twist to these scrapbook pages.

A SMILING COVER

▶ Make a 12-inch-diameter circular wood book (page 78) with black album pages to fit.

• Enlarge the pattern (page 50) for the smile design (page 216). Use the pattern to cut a stencil (page 64).

• Prime the covers, let them dry, then paint them (both sides and the edges) yellow. Let dry. Stencil on the eyes and the mouth in black. Let dry and assemble the book.

> ❝Reflect that life is composed of small inci-dents and petty occurrences.❞
>
> —SAMUEL JOHNSON

YOU WILL NEED:

❋ Basic supplies (page 42)

Supplies for this scrapbook:

❋ 1/4" birch plywood

❋ Large notebook rings

❋ Acid-free black paper for album pages

❋ Black and yellow paint for cover

❋ Paint primer

❋ Paintbrush

❋ Objects to color-copy (such as embroidered smile patch, candy, buttons, and trinkets)

❋ Acid-free paper (stationery) in white and assorted bright colors

❋ Decorative paper punch (we used heart-shaped)

❋ Black marker

❋ White single-ply illustration board

Copying 3-D and Other Decorations

Try to plan for the photocopies you will need, and make them—and a few extras—all at one time.

Throughout the book, color photocopies of 3-D objects are used for page decorations. To copy these, first remove all photographs and flat pieces. Arrange the 3-D objects on a piece of white illustration board, glue the objects in position (see below), and color-copy (page 67). Color-copy the smile patch separately, adjusting sizes as needed.

A SMILING BROTHER AND SISTER

▲ On a piece of white board, use a compass to draw a circle ⅛ inch smaller all around than the page. Arrange the candy letters and decorate with other candy and buttons.

• Follow the instructions for photocopying 3-D objects from "Copying 3-D and Other Decorations" box, above right.

• Cut the circle out of the copy paper. Make a small slit in the page to tuck under one corner of the photograph, to keep it from hiding the decoration.

• Arrange and attach the pieces following the photograph and "Making a Collage" on page 85.

OVAL CANDY FRAME

············◆············

▶ Crop the photograph (or photo-copy) to an oval shape (page 65).

• Center the oval on a piece of yellow paper and lightly trace around it. Remove the picture.

• On the paper draw a larger oval 1³/₈ inches beyond the marked picture edge. Cut out the larger oval. Using decorative paper edgers (page 57), cut away the center oval to make a mat for the photograph.

• In the same manner, draw the edge of the picture oval on a piece of white paper. Then draw two larger ovals, the first ³/₈ inch beyond the marked pic-ture edge, and the second 2 inches beyond that, to form an oval border.

• Arrange the heart-shaped buttons or candy on the oval border as shown; glue in place and color-copy.

• Cut out the copy along the outer edge, using paper edgers. Cut away the center, leaving a 2-inch-wide decorated border.

• Using paper punches (page 59), punch evenly spaced holes around the inner border edge and hearts around the outer edge.

• Center the inner yellow mat (made earlier) on a piece of pink paper and lightly trace around the outer edge. Remove the mat. On the pink paper, draw a large oval 1 ¹/₂ inches beyond the marked mat edge.

• Using the paper edgers, cut along the outer oval line. Using regular scis-sors, cut out the center, leaving a 1 ¹/₂-inch-wide border that will just fit around the yellow mat.

• Cut out a yellow oval ¹/₂ inch larger all around than the outer edge of the pink border, using paper edgers.

• Arrange the pieces, centering the photograph on the large yellow oval, then adding both the pink and yellow borders, topped with the candy border. Follow the photograph and "Making a Collage" to attach.

> ❝The highlight of my childhood was making my brother laugh so hard that food came out his nose.❞
>
> —GARRISON KEILLOR

A BIG SMILE

▲ Cut a yellow circle to fit the album page.

• Using the stencil you made for the cover, lightly draw the outline of the mouth and eyes onto the yellow circle.

• With an X-acto knife, carefully cut out the shapes.

•. With spray adhesive, attach the yellow face to the black page.

SMILING FACES HAPPY PLACES

▲ Photocopy the printed happy-face pattern, so that it measures about 4 3/4 inches across. Use the copied pattern to cut a stencil.

• With a compass draw a 4 3/4-inch-diameter circle on five different colors of paper. Use the stencil and a black marker to mark the eyes and smile on each circle. Cut out the circles.

• Cut two yellow paper rectangles, each 1/16 inch larger all around than the photographs.

• Photocopy as many sunflower paper corner mounts (page 201) as

you need for your photographs. Cut, fold, and glue them; color, if you wish.

• Color-copy the happy-face patch several times, and cut out the circles with decorative paper edgers to use as page decorations.

• Follow the photograph and "Making a Collage" to attach.

JOSH'S FIRST SCRAPBOOK

Whether it's collecting leaves on a bright fall day or cutting out their favorite magazine pictures, endless creative possibilities exist for children. Making a scrapbook is a natural activity for these exuberant collectors. In their own albums children can treasure their own drawings, photographs, and mementos, and in so doing also learn the importance of savoring their personal and family history. (Parents can also augment the child's book with items that they consider worth saving.) This rugged wooden scrapbook—shaped like a briefcase with its own little handle—while not indestructible, will certainly take the inevitable blows of childhood better than most. And the handle makes for easy transport to show-and-tell, or to grandma's house.

YOU WILL NEED:

- ❈ Basic supplies (page 42)
- Supplies for this scrapbook:
- ❈ 1/4" birch plywood
- ❈ Scrap of wood, 1/2" thick, for handle
- ❈ Two 2" notebook rings
- ❈ Acid-free paper in rainbow colors (red, orange, yellow, green, blue, violet, magenta) and black and brown for cover and page decorations
- ❈ Gold metal semicircular clips (or gold paper disks cut in half)
- ❈ Primer and paint in white and brown
- ❈ Permanent black-ink marker

HAVE COVER, WILL TRAVEL

▲ Following the directions for "Wood Books" (page 78), cut 9" x 12" covers, rounding the corners and drilling two holes, 4 inches apart, centered 1/2 inch below the top edge.

• From the scrap plywood, cut a U-shaped handle, making it 1 inch wide, with the outer edges measuring 5 inches across and about 2 inches from top to bottom. Drill a hole 1/2 inch in from the edge at the center of each of the arm ends.

• Prime, then paint, the inner surface of the front and both surfaces of the back in white. Let dry between coats.

Paint the edges on all sides, as well as the handles, in brown.

• Using spray adhesive, cover the outer surface of the front with black paper. Glue on a 5/8-inch brown border with square corners extending beyond the rounded wood corners. Attach gold clips (or gold paper half–discs) overlapped as shown, to each corner.

• Cover the flat surfaces of the handle with brown paper. Use a black marker to draw a line of alternating dots and dashes 1/4 inch in from the outer edge of the handle and centered on the cover border strips (to simulate stitching).

• Enlarge the patterns (page 50) for the alphabet to fit the child's name

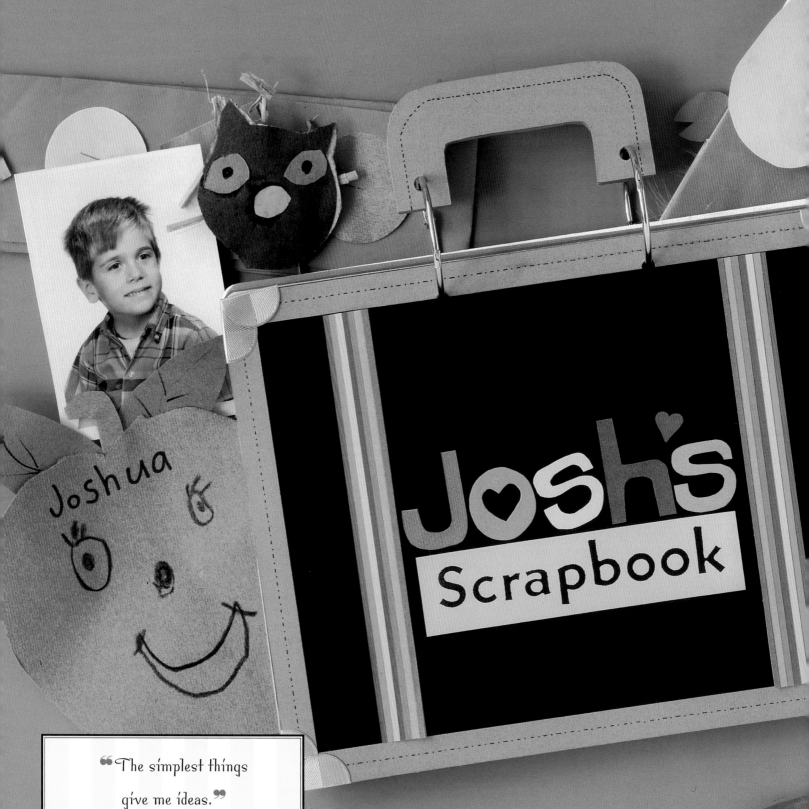

Joshua

Josh's
Scrapbook

between the strips and again to spell "Scrapbook." Cut the rainbow-colored letters for the name.

• Photocopy "Scrapbook" letters onto yellow paper and cut them out in a 1 ½-inch-wide strip. Glue the yellow strip in place.

• Make two rainbow strips 9 inches long, starting with a ⅞-inch-wide strip of red. Add the colors in rainbow order, making each strip ⅛ inch narrower than the previous one, ending with a ⅛-inch-wide strip. Glue the layers together, keeping one long edge even and the other edge in colored steps. With the straight edge toward the center, place a strip on each side of the letters; trim the strip ends at the brown border strips. Glue the rainbow strips in place.

• Create album pages to fit (page 54). With an X-acto knife, cut tiny X's in the paper directly over the drilled holes on the handle and the cover. Assemble the book with the notebook rings.

THE FACE-PAINT BOOK

There is a magical quality to certain days of childhood—particularly when there are a group of children and a grown-up ready to play too. This bright and cheerful scrapbook reflects the mood of one such festive afternoon during a block party. Here's an album in which whimsical elements, including a tiger's head, a snake, and a star, are cleverly combined with the photographs and page designs. Remember, there is usually more than enough material in the photographs themselves for lively and innovative page layouts.

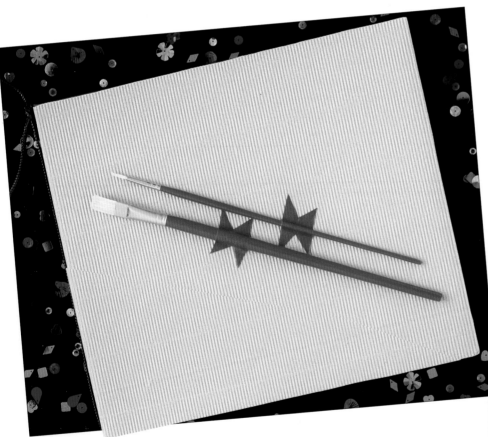

• Cut the paper cover a little larger than the album cover. Using spray adhesive, attach the paper to the album, covering the folded-over edges of the tape. Lifting the edges up slightly, trim the paper cover edges to match the album cover, and press back in place. Complete your album, following Steps 3 through 5 of the Basic Book.

• We attached paint brushes to our cover, but you can use your imagination and invent your own design element.

YOU WILL NEED:

❧ Basic supplies (page 42)
Supplies for this scrapbook:
❧ Mat board or foam core board, 1/8" thick
❧ Card stock
❧ Paper for cover and liner
❧ Paper for album pages
❧ Tape for covering edges
❧ Decorative cord, 1/8" diameter
❧ Acid-free paper (store-bought or handmade) in assorted colors
❧ Novelty paper

DESIGN-YOUR-OWN COVER
·········◆·········

▲ Following the directions for the Basic Book on page 69, cut and join book covers (ours are 10" x 11"), allowing for a thicker spine if you are using foam core board. Cover the cut edges of each cover board with tape, folding the tape over the edges and trimming to make neat corners.

of the yellow border, making the point edges ⅛ inch smaller.

• Glue the layers together and mount the photograph at the center. (In all albums, glue the paper pieces with neutral-pH adhesive and use photo-mount squares to attach photographs.)

• Crop the small photograph (page 65) of the star-painted hand to a star shape and mount it on matching-shaped colored papers, cutting each underlying layer ⅛ inch larger than the previous layer.

MADAM PAINTER

▲ The bright pink and glittery gold background papers echo the bright, festive colors in the photograph, as well as the carefree carnival atmosphere suggested by the jester cap. The random black stripes are reminiscent of the design on the painter's blouse. Check your photographs for similar colors and designs to repeat.

BE A STAR

▼ To make the large pointed frame, cut a yellow paper rectangle 2 inches larger than the photograph. Working freehand, cut out 2-inch-deep wedges to make the many-pointed border.

• Using the yellow piece as a guide, cut a black piece with a pointed border ⅛ inch larger all around than the yellow piece. Alternating red and aqua, cut a triangle to fit each point

BE A CAT

▼ Using a photocopying machine, enlarge a small detail—the cat's face on the child's cheek, for example, making the copy about 4 inches long. (The paintbrush, also a picture detail, was cut from colored paper in a size appropriate to the enlarged cat face.)

THE BASEBALL BOOK

A boy, a great team, and his inspiring coach are all the elements you need for a perfect Little League day— one to remember forever in a scrapbook shaped like a baseball itself.

YOU WILL NEED:

❖ Basic supplies (page 42)

Supplies for this scrapbook:

❖ 1/4" birch plywood

❖ 2 large notebook rings

❖ Acid-free black paper for album pages

❖ Acid-free colored paper for page decorations

❖ Primer

❖ White, black, and red paint

❖ Acetate for stencil and photo cropper

❖ Colored pencils, markers, or crayons

MAKE THE CATCH

◄ Enlarge and photocopy the line art for the baseball glove, shown on page 217, onto tan paper (or enlarge onto white paper and color it with colored pencils, markers, or crayons). Cut out the glove copy, then cut out the ball on the glove to make a mat opening for the photograph.

COVER THE BALL

▲ Make a wood book with 8-inch-diameter round covers (page 78); prime and paint it white. Enlarge the pattern (page 50) for the baseball, shown on page 218, and cut separate stencils from acetate (page 64) for the seam lines and stitches. Paint the seam lines black and the stitches red. Let dry between colors. Cut black album pages to fit (page 54), and assemble.

► Make a collage.

THE ROLLERBLADE BOOK

The Rollerblader's laced-up skates are echoed in the construction of this scrapbook. Panels from an old Rollerblade box were used to make the album itself. Here's a perfect example of how you can make a handmade book out of material lying around the house.

YOU WILL NEED:

❖ Basic supplies (page 42)

Supplies for this scrapbook:

❖ Box with printed design and/or words appropriate to theme of book (we used a rollerblade box) for cover

❖ Acid-free paper (stationery) in assort-ed colors to coordinate with printed box for cover liner and album pages

❖ Satin ribbon, 1/4" wide, for lacing

❖ Contrasting-colored ribbon for tie

❖ Yarn needle for lacing

A LACED-UP COVER

▲ Deacidify a printed rollerblade box and use it to make a 9" x 9" laced scrapbook (page 74), cutting the box for the cover, lining the inside covers with acid-free paper, and lacing with the ribbons, attaching the ribbon ends with a dab of glue (rather than knot-ting them). Cut the album pages (page 54), alternating the colors.

A DAY IN THE LACES

◀ Use the album for your photographs of any sport theme. Use acid-free glue to hold the paper pieces in place, and use photo-mount squares to attach the photographs.

> ❝ Imagination is more important than knowledge. ❞
>
> —ALBERT EINSTEIN

A HOUSEWARMING

The uniqueness of this scrapbook can only be produced by hand. A piece of brightly painted wood in the shape of a house, with windows peeking onto photographs of a warm, inviting interior, pays tribute to the comforts of home. The "four walls" of this album can be used to document a move to a new house, to remember the house where you or your children were born, or to collect photographs and memorabilia from every house you've ever lived in.

WINDOWS ON YOUR WORLD

▶ Enlarge the pattern (page 221) for the house shape. Following the directions for "The Wood Books," page 78, make the house-shaped cover, cutting out the windows, and make album-shaped pages to fit (page 54). Prime and paint the book blue or give it a natural finish with polyurethane spray.

THERE'S NO PLACE LIKE HOME

▶ Inside the book, simply mount the pictures of the home interior with photo-mount squares. This album makes a wonderful housewarming gift for a new homeowner or a keepsake for someone about to move.

YOU WILL NEED:

❋ Basic supplies (page 42)

Supplies for this scrapbook:

❋ 1/4" birch plywood
❋ 2 large notebook rings
❋ Acid-free multicolored paper for album pages
❋ Primer and paint for cover or clear polyurethane spray
❋ Photo-mount squares

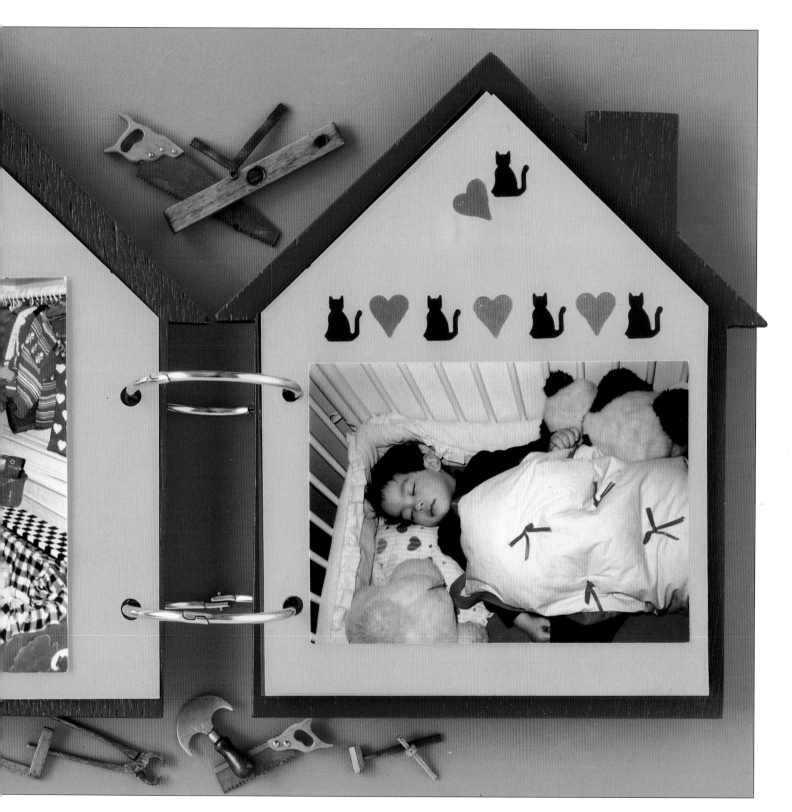

"Who ran to help me when I fell,
And would some pretty story tell,
Or kiss the place and make it well?
My mother."

—Ann Taylor

Love

SPECIAL DAYS

Not only holidays, but those special "first" days, are the bright high-lights of our lives. From them we draw warm and precious memories. We also enjoy holidays as opportunities to build and express love and the pleasures of family and community. Unpack those photographs and mementos and feel the magic all over again. We can relive our lives all year round by putting together scrapbooks that are radiant with all the excite-ment, warmth, and tradition that special days, from Christmas to Valentine's Day—and even a child's first day back at school— can offer us.

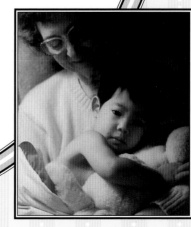

The Joy of Creation

Inside this album the pages are brightly decorated with easy-to-make trims. Some pages have interactive parts, such as the gift boxes which can be opened, making the book fun to create and a joy to look through. Many decorative frames and mounts have been used to accent individual, gemlike moments.

This is a good book for children to participate in preparing (with adult assistance for younger children).

CHRISTMAS REFLECTIONS

Aside from its religious associations, Christmas is a time to give gifts, not just the store-bought kind, but the gifts we give of ourselves: our time, our care, and our celebration of tradition. Herein lie the great memories that live on in our children, our friends, and all our loved ones. These memories need not flee. All the care and attention we put into making a Christmas can live on in the love we put into creating our memory album.

COVERED WITH CHEER

▲ Cover the album (page 52) with one fabric and use a different fabric for the liners. Cut a piece of the liner fabric and, using spray adhesive, attach it to cover the first page (facing the front inside cover), trimming the edges to match the album page.

YOU WILL NEED:

- Basic supplies (page 42)

Supplies for this scrapbook:
- Small album with 5 ³/₄" x 8" pages
- Holiday-print fabrics for cover and liner
- Acid-free papers in red, green, and gold
- Large rubber stamp with "Merry Christmas" design
- Green ink pad
- Narrow ribbon
- Gold photo corners
- Decorative paper punches with star and heart designs
- Decorative paper edgers

HEART OF MY HEART

▲ Color-photocopy (page 67) the clip-art heart on page 190. Cut the rectangle from the copy with paper edgers (page 57), and use scissors to cut out the center of the heart to make the mat opening.

• Position the photograph behind the opening and use acid-free tape to hold it in place. Place the framed picture on the page, and pencil-mark the placement of each corner edge. Remove the picture and glue the gold photograph corners at the marked spots. Slip the framed picture into place.

Scattered Stars

A scattering of punched-out stars in Christmas colors will give your album a bright, festive look.

This frame, and other Christmas clip art frames, can be photocopied from page 190.

MERRY CHRISTMAS

▲ Cut a red rectangle using the paper edger. Cut gold and green papers, making each layer 1/4 inch smaller than the previous layer. Glue the layers together.

• Stamp "Merry Christmas" on a piece of white paper or handwrite your own message. Trim the paper to a rectangle to fit on the layered papers. Glue in place.

• Cut the background from a photograph (or color-copy), leaving the silhouette. Mount in place and sprinkle with a scattering of stars, punched out with a decorative paper

FABULOUS FRAMES

▲ Color photocopy the clip-art frames on page 190; cut out the copied frames and the inside window. Glue the narrow frame to green paper and cut around the inner and outer edges, leaving about 1/8 inch of color showing. Tape the photographs to the frames and glue to the page, adding glue only to the paper (not the photographs).

• Add a name tag and scattered stars for trim.

THE GIFT BOX

▶ Cut a green paper strip about 3 inches wide. Fold it in half crosswise. Holding the fold at the top, fold the end of the front strip back up, making this second fold about a half inch below the center fold. Repeat with the back strip, enclosing the center-fold lip between the strip ends.

• Cut away the background of a photograph (or color copy), leaving just the figure silhouette. Mount the lower edge of the photograph on the folded lip, so that it pops up when the card is opened. Trim off the excess strip ends to leave a box shape that conceals the photograph when the card is closed.

• Cut a 15-inch length of ribbon and glue it to the vertical center of the back with the ribbon ends extended. Glue the back of the box to the page. Tie the ribbon ends into a bow, trimming any excess.

• Punch out red and gold stars; glue them to the box front.

• Add "Do Not Open Until Dec. 25" to the box.

CHRISTMAS TREE & SURPRISE BOX

▼ Trace the full-size tree pattern on page 208 and cut it out. Use it to draw the shape onto green paper. Cut out the tree.

• Trace and cut out a gold star. Punch out several hearts from red paper and glue them to the tree; glue on the star. Fold the tree in half lengthwise (decorated side in), and glue the underside of the left half to the page.

• Cut a 3" x 5" rectangle of red paper; fold it in half to form a card.

• Using paper edgers, cut a green rectangle to fit inside the card. Glue this to the center of the inner right half of the card.

• Crop a photograph (page 65) to about 2 inches square and mount it, centered, over the green paper inside the card.

• Punch two small hole near the front edge of the card. Thread a 15-inch length of ribbon through the holes and tie them into a bow. Trim the ends. Glue the back of the card to the page at the lower right of the folded tree (folded edge of the card is next to the fold of the tree). Fold the right half of the tree over the box and glue it in place.

• Add an inscription tag mounted on gold with a red punched-out star saying, "CHRISTMAS IS FULL OF SURPRISES!"

> ❝ Your own gift can present every moment with the cumulative force of a whole life's cultivation. ❞
>
> —RALPH WALDO EMERSON

▼ Mount a photograph on a red rectangle, leaving a ¼-inch border. Add scattered red, green, and gold star punchouts.

VALENTINE GIFT BOOKS

Consisting of little more than eight to twelve pages, these charming books can contain anything: poems, snapshots, love letters, or tiny portraits. Here, a hand holding a heart in its palm with a string tied around its finger (so as not to forget), and a simple heart bound with twine, produce a dramatic effect with very little effort. And remember, a simple handmade book like this is not limited to Valentine's Day but can be given any time that loving feeling strikes you.

PAPER HEART BOOK

▾ Enlarge the pattern (page 50) for the paper heart on page 204. Fold the red paper in half and with the left (fold) edge of the pattern along the paper fold, trace around the pattern on the red paper. Cut out a heart for the cover.

• Cut four evenly spaced notches along the folded edge as shown, then cut several random notches on the remaining edges, if desired.

• Trim away ¼-inch around the outer (nonfold) edges of the cover pattern to make a template for the album pages.

• Folding the white paper in half as you did for the cover, use the template to cut out the double-heart pages, cutting four, or as many as you need.

• Cut four notches along each page fold to correspond to the cover holes. Lay the opened pages over the opened cover, matching the fold-line holes.

• Thread the cord ends through the inner set of holes from the outside cover to the page center. Tie the ends at the center to secure the pages to the cover, then thread one end back out through the top hole and the other through the bottom hole. Close the book, wrap the cord ends around the heart at the edge notches, if desired, and tie the ends in a bow.

YOU WILL NEED:

❧ Basic supplies (page 42)

Supplies for this scrapbook:

❧ Acid-free textured red paper

❧ Acid-free white paper for album pages

❧ Cord for tying pages and wrapping heart

YOU WILL NEED:

- ❈ Basic supplies (page 42)

  Supplies for this scrapbook:
- ❈ Bristol board for cover and album pages
- ❈ Acid-free red paper for hearts
- ❈ Cord for tying pages and wrapping
- ❈ Acetate or sturdy clear plastic bag for photo cropper

PAPER HAND BOOK

▶ Enlarge the patterns (page 50) for the hand and the heart-shaped pages on page 204. Fold a sheet of bristol board in half and, matching the pattern-fold edge to the paper fold, trace around the hand pattern. Cut out the shape for the covers, cutting out the heart shape on the front cover.

• In the same manner, matching the fold edges, cut out several double pages. Cut out one heart from red paper. Glue the heart to the first-page heart. Use a single-hole paper punch to make two evenly spaced holes about an inch apart along the fold of each page and the cover.

• Place the opened pages over the opened cover, matching the holes. Thread the cord ends through the holes from the outside cover to the center page; tie the ends at the center to secure the pages to the cover.

• Bringing the cord ends to the outside, close the book and wrap the cord ends around the hand as shown; tie in a bow around the forefinger.

BACK TO SCHOOL

Who can forget the excitement and anticipation of the first day of school? And while you think you may never forget such feelings, little details—what you wore, who your schoolbus companions were, and what your teacher really looked like—may indeed have slid into oblivion. But this needn't be the case for your children. A Back to School Scrapbook can keep these marvelous details vivid and tangible. This album has made innovative use of such motifs as the picket fence, carrying it into the design of the pages themselves. The use of colors matching those in the photograph and a simple but effective page trim makes this album worthy of an A+.

COVER YOUR BOOKS

▲ Following the directions for the Traditional Book on page 72, make a 9" x 11¹/₂" scrapbook.

• Make album pages (page 54).

PICKET FENCE

▶ You can use the picket fence shown in the photograph as a design motif by cutting simple fence strips from white paper to extend the fence across the whole page. If you have a similar photograph of a child leaving for the first day of school, study your picture for background or architectural details you can use—if not a white picket fence, then perhaps a duplicate door frame or arch

can frame the whole picture. Any shrubs, trees, or sidewalk blocks in the picture also make memorable decorations.

• Throughout your book, glue the paper pieces in place with acid-free glue and use photo-mount squares to attach the photographs.

YOU WILL NEED:

❈ Basic supplies (page 42)

Supplies for this scrapbook:

❈ Mat board or foam core board, 1/8" thick.

❈ Acid-free card stock

❈ Fabric for cover

❈ Paper for liner

❈ Narrow ribbon or decorative cord

❈ Acid-free paper (stationery) for album pages

❈ Acid-free paper in assorted colors

❈ White pencil or marker

OFF TO SCHOOL!

·············◆·············

▼ To create the back of the school bus, cut yellow paper pieces to fit the proportions of the front of the bus as shown in the photograph. Cut the strip and wheels from black paper and add cut-out silhouettes or circles showing the faces of schoolmates.

• You can decorate your school bus photographs in this manner, completing the bus with the sections not shown (as we did), or duplicating the whole bus. The face photos can be cut from actual photographs or color photocopies.

• You can use this design concept to display your children's school photographs. You can also use them to make pages of your own classroom or after-school activity scenes, using colored paper to create the desired background and details.

It's All in the Details

To design the pages of this book, we used shapes and themes that appear in the individual photographs. While your own school pictures may be similar to these, the details will probably differ. We suggest, therefore, that you adapt the decorations rather than try to duplicate them exactly.

Josh meets his teacher and new classmates!

Have a Nice School Day!

PAPER DOLLS OF CHILDHOOD

·············◆·············

▲ Paper-doll chains, even if not directly related to a photograph, echo the broad theme of groups of children. They are an especially wonderful embellishment for pictures of playgrounds or group activities.

TO MAKE THE PAPER-DOLL CHAINS:

• Cut a long strip of 2 1/2-inch-wide colored paper.

• Enlarge the pattern (page 50) for the paper dolls on page 219, and cut out the pattern shape.

• Measure the width of your pattern from one flat edge (center of doll) to the opposite flat edge. Fold the colored strip the exact width of your pattern,

making a series of accordion pleats. Press each fold with your thumbnail to make a sharp crease.

• Trace the pattern onto the top layer, matching the flat edges of the pattern to the paper folds.

• Keeping the strip tightly folded, cut out along the pattern outline, cutting through all layers at the same time. Unfold the chain and cut away the incomplete dolls at each end.

LARGE PAPER DOLL

·············◆·············

▲ The enlarged single doll was taken from the paper-doll chain. A small red heart and a head silhouette were added.

• To make the large doll, enlarge the pattern of the paper doll 225 percent

> " How dear to this heart
> are the scenes of my childhood,
> when fond recollection
> presents them to view! "
>
> —SAMUEL WOODWORTH

and use it to cut out a single whole boy or girl doll from colored paper. Add a child's face cut from a photograph.

• Tip: Try tucking one leg of the doll under or over the photograph with an arm extending over the picture to make the doll appear to interact with the child in the picture.

• Add sunny phrases to the pages.

A GIFT FOR MOTHER

While a festive floral bouquet is often de rigueur for Mom in May, now you can supplement your Mother's Day arrangement with the gift of memory that she will cherish forever. This vibrant bouquet of paper flowers is made even more cheerful with the use of primary colors and black faux stitching, a bevy of blooms that feature the faces of loved ones, and a treasure trove of love notes or other memorabilia. An unexpected treat for a deserving Mom.

rotating the layers as desired allowing the petals to fold forward; glue the stack to the red square.

• From bristol board or card stock, cut album pages to fit your binder (page 54), making holes with the three-hole punch.

COVER STITCH

▲ Following "How to Create a Random-Torn Edge" on page 56, tear a square of red paper to fit the cover. Glue it to the front of the binder, leaving just the edges of the paper free all around.

• Enlarge the patterns (page 50) for all the layers shown on page 207. With small scissors, cut the flowers and the circle from different colors of paper. Fold the petals of the flowers forward. Lightly pencil-mark the detail lines on the two larger flowers as indicated on the patterns.

• Machine-stitch or "faux-sew" (using a black marker to draw broken lines) the detail lines on the two larger flowers.

• Starting with the largest flower, glue the centers of the flowers together,

YOU WILL NEED:

- ❀ Basic supplies (page 42)
- <u>Supplies for this scrapbook:</u>
- ❀ Black paper-covered notebook binder
- ❀ Sheets of acid-free white two-ply bristol board or card stock for album pages
- ❀ Acid-free paper (regular or handmade) in assorted colors
- ❀ Blank note card or flat piece of card stock
- ❀ Three-hole paper punch
- ❀ Sewing machine (optional)
- ❀ Black and red sewing thread (optional)
- ❀ Black and red fine-point markers
- ❀ Decorative paper edge scissors

SUNNY-FACE FLOWERS

▼ Enlarge the following patterns on pages 205–207: the two smaller flowers, two leaves, and two butterflies. Cut four sets of flowers in different colors. Cut four sets of green leaves and four strips for stems.

THEY SPELL MOTHER

▲ Cut a yellow paper rectangle to fit your album page.

• Enlarge the patterns (page 50) for the C corner on page 205. Cut four sets of corners from three different-colored papers.

• Lightly glue the corner layers together and stitch or "faux-sew" the detail line. Glue the corners to the yellow paper.

• Enlarge the letter patterns needed to spell MOTHER (page 197). Cut each letter from a different-colored paper. Following the photograph, arrange and tape the letters onto the note card. (For "faux-sewing" only, glue the letters in place.)

• Lightly pencil-mark a random stitching line, making sure all the letters will be sewn through. Open the notecard and stitch or "faux-sew" the guideline over the letters on the top half of the card. Write a message on the inside of the card.

• Glue the card to the yellow paper, then glue the yellow paper to the album page.

Alphabet design by Shanyn Prentiss.

• Using paper edgers (page 57), cut two small rectangles (about 2" x 2 ½") from aqua paper and two slightly smaller rectangles from white paper. With regular scissors, cut two black strips for signposts. Cut the butterfly from different colors.

• Carefully crop your photographs or photocopies (page 65) to fit the square space at the center of each small flower.

• Machine-stitch or "faux-sew" the lines on the flowers, butterfly, and name signs, following the printed patterns.

• Arrange and attach the paper cutouts on the album page, following the photograph and "Making a Collage," page 85.

• Add the names and ages of the children, or other messages, to the signs with the markers.

Sewing Paper

To machine-stitch through paper layers, set machine to sew about 10 stitches per inch. Do not use too fine a stitch.

BIRDS OF A FEATHER BIRTHDAY ALBUM

What better way to express heartfelt gratitude on a friend's birthday than to create a gift scrapbook that documents all the funny, memorable moments that define a great relationship. The pages of this scrapbook are filled with photographs of two good friends as they "flock together" over the years: the day they met, at the beach, and sharing an intimate moment of conversation.

CLOSE COVER

·············◆·············

▲ Use a scrap of wood veneer to cut out a rectangular frame for a picture of best friends, trimming it with gold semicircular clips and mounting it on a larger rectangle of colored paper that has been cut with paper edgers (page 57).

• Use the white pencil to write "Birds of a Feather" on a small strip of black paper cut with decorative edgers. Add the beaded feathers. Arrange the pieces following the photograph and "Making a Collage" on page 85 to complete the cover.

• Decorate the inside pages simply with only a few embellishments.

QUIET MOMENTS

▼ These simple, quiet pages each feature a single photograph mounted on colored paper that has been cut with paper edgers (page 57).

• Add a few embellishments like the paper leaf (use an actual leaf as a pattern) and a heart trinket, as we used on the left page.

• Cut a decorative edge on the photograph itself (right page), then use photo-mount squares to attach it to the colored paper. Glue the unit to the album page with pH neutral glue.

YOU WILL NEED:

❋ Basic supplies (page 42)

Supplies for this scrapbook:

❋ Photograph album

❋ Scrap of wood veneer

❋ Acid-free paper in assorted colors for cover and page decoration

❋ Two feathers with glued-on beads

❋ Gold semicircular clips (or use gold notary seals cut in half)

❋ White pencil (photograph marker)

❋ Decorative-edge scissors

❝ A friend may well be reckoned the masterpiece of nature. ❞

—RALPH WALDO EMERSON

TRAVEL TREASURES

O ur voyages, be they to far-flung continents or to simple, local country retreats, are always chockful of memorable moments. We are relaxed, the scenery is beautiful, and, often, we are surrounded by our family and friends. And we all tend to shoot a mountain of photographs that might give a Himalayan trekker pause. It's what happens afterwards that makes for trouble in paradise: a dozen boxes and bags of our precious memories languishing, unappreciated, in a dark corner of a closet. Here are a few tried-and-true suggestions that will inspire scrapbooks for your closeted cache—as exciting and memorable as the vacation itself!

California

ALCATRAZ

Wine Tours

AUGUST 22

The day begins bright and early so we can drive
north to the WINE COUNTRY!

We take a tour of William Hill Winery. First we
sample grapes right off the vine and then we get
to see how the wine is made. We also get to taste
a selection of both white and red wines.

We continue touring the area and stop for lunch at
Mustard's. The best lunch so far.

We spend the rest of the day driving through both
Napa and Sonoma valleys.

We end the day with a casual dinner in Chinatown.

Chinatown Then & Now

California

DRINKING IT ALL IN

▲ Note the use of the postcard, with the pictures cut out and the remaining border with place name used to frame the photograph. This is an easy way to attach the vacationers to the place visited. The cut-out postcard picture (the grapes) is also part of the page collage.

• Use appropriately colored paper to form a unifying backdrop to the collection of memorabilia on a page. If you missed taking a photograph at a particular spot, you can place people there anyway by cutting their silhouettes from any photograph, then photocopying and placing them on a postcard or another of your own photographs. This has the added advantage of eliminating any unwanted background in the original picture.

The Big Picture

This scrapbook uses quite a bit of travel memorabilia in addition to personal photographs. In such a case it's best to plan your cover first and then design your inside pages to match the cover. This gives you a great opportunity to determine the theme, color, and style of your interior pages. The pages shown offer a few ideas, but the real creativity is in your own hands.

SOMEWHERE IN ECUADOR

A rusted horseshoe, a handmade silver bracelet, a small tin sun, and a few pieces of hand-woven cloth summon up the colors and textures of Latin America in this album. Little inexpensive trinkets and swatches of colorful ethnic textiles can be color-photocopied and used as backgrounds, unique borders, and accents if inventively trimmed. When putting together this scrapbook of a trip to rural Ecuador, we found that the photographs that worked best were often the most unassuming ones—candid shots of a meal, a child at play with a stick and hoop, the interior of a humble bedroom. Like the photocopied mementos, they filled the album with the mood of the trip's people and places.

book. Because many of the fabrics we used were striped, it was easy to cut strips from the paper color copies for borders, using paper edgers (page 57).

• A page-sized piece of color-copied textile provides the unifying backdrop to this collage. Copies of 3-D ornaments and strips of fabric add further interest to the mounted pieces. Attach the pieces in place,

following "Making a Collage" on page 85.

• The travelogue was created on a computer and printed on special paper, but you can also use a type-writer, show off your calligraphy, or use your best penmanship to tell your story and record your comments.

• A textured-paper background was used for the collage on the right-hand page, below.

COVERING THE WORLD

·······◆·······

▲ A simple photograph, cropped to a square (page 65) and slipped into a protective acetate sleeve (page 56), also cropped square, was mounted on a piece of textured paper, cut ¼ inch larger all around than the photograph.

TELLING YOUR STORY

·······◆·······

▶ Make a number of copies of the fabrics and ornaments on a color photo-copier (page 67) to use throughout the

A NATURAL TRANQUILITY

············◆············

▲ On this quiet page, the placement of photographs showing the natural beauty of Ecuador greatly varies the look.

•Each of the two vertical photographs has a top and bottom border strip cut with paper edgers from a color photocopy of a textile.

THE VARIETY OF LIFE

············◆············

▲ Although this spread has many pictures, their symmetrical arrangement over rough-textured paper, and the uniform use of the color-copied braid ribbon that stretches across the pages between the photographs, gives it a sense of focus, balance, and interest.

PATTERNS AND PEOPLE

············◆············

▼ A single photograph with a wide border makes a dramatic page, highlighting a very special photograph. Simply mount the picture in the center of a color-copied piece of fabric, cutting the copy about 3 inches larger all around than the photograph, using paper edgers for cutting.

YOU WILL NEED:

❋ Basic supplies (page 42)

Supplies for this scrapbook:

❋ Spiral bound photograph album (ours was 14" x 14")

❋ Regional textiles and 3-D objects to color-copy (such as trinkets, souvenir jewelry, and coins)

❋ Acid-free paper (store-bought or handmade, in assorted theme-related colors)

❋ Textured paper

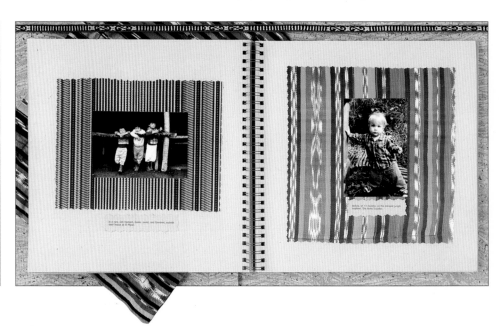

It's Gotta Have Rhythm

It's important to establish a rhythm to the pages, such as going from a powerful layout to several calm ones, and then back to a powerful one again.

After lunch with Lupe and Osvaldo and Guido on the hill behind El Placer. After having been away for a year and a half, our shower is still there (upper right), but has grown a bit rickety. Bolivia is pointing down to the horses playing below. She loves being on the farm and gets extremely dirty as quick as she possibly can. Lupe is five months pregnant, but Osvaldo doesn't tell us until later.

Memories of our Cloudforest Home

GOOD DOG

MINIATURE JACK RUSSELL TERRIER

Jackie

BORN JANUARY 11 1996

"A dog is the only thing on earth that loves you more than you love yourself."

—Josh Billings

ANIMAL FRIENDS

If dogs—and don't forget cats and horses—are man's best friends, surely they deserve to have their most glorious moments immortalized in a scrapbook. What about a special show dog that travels to competitions all over the country? Or a horse that has taught a youngster the true meaning of discipline and caring? Or a special scruffy kitten, now turned into a cat, whose loving heart is as big as her enormous furry girth? Our animal companions generate so much love—more than can ever be contained in a single album. Here are a few scrapbooks that endeavor to capture the loving nature of the beast.

HORSE SHOW

his regal equine head, handmade of wood veneer over black foam core, makes for a fitting scrapbook tribute to a young boy's first horse show. The photographs inside depict the various stages of horse care, preparation, and the show itself, as well as the beginning rider aglow with his accomplishments. Other memorabilia can include show programs, ribbons, and certificates, even little trinkets from the riding outfit or the horse's gear. While we haven't made extensive use of commercially made stickers, this seemed a perfect opportunity to introduce some. These are from Mrs. Grossman's enormous variety of thoughtfully designed, high-quality stickers.

HORSE-SHAPED COVER

◄ Enlarge the pattern (page 50) for the horse's head on page 220.

• Follow Steps 7 through 10 of "The Foam Board Books" on page 80, to cut out and bevel the spine edges.

• Tape the enlarged pattern on the wrong side of the veneer. With an X-acto knife and fresh blade, cut out a rough outline, making it slightly larger than the pattern. Flip the pattern over and rough-cut another (reversed) piece. Spray the underside of one veneer piece with spray adhesive and, positioning it carefully, press it onto the corresponding foam core album cover; attach the other veneer piece to the other cover. (The spine is left uncovered.)

• Using the X-acto knife, carefully trim the veneer edges to match the foam-board shape. Use spray polyurethane to finish the veneer covers.

• Using the pattern for the horse head as a template, cut separate shaped album pages

from black paper (page 54), joining them with black tape along the straight part of the spine edge.

• To assemble the book, open the pages flat at the center seam and lay them over the opened cover (veneer side down). Cut a length of ribbon and lay it along the center seam; close the book and tie the ribbon ends in a bow along the outside of the spine. Leaving long ends, trim off any excess ribbon.

• Decorate the cover with a prize ribbon, if desired.

YOU WILL NEED:

- - - - - - - - - - - - - - - - - - - -

❧ Basic supplies (page 42)

Supplies for this scrapbook:

❧ Black foam core board, 3/16" thick

❧ Sheet of wood veneer for cover

❧ Acid-free black paper for album pages

❧ 1" wide black masking tape (from art-supply or photo-supply store)

❧ Ribbon for tie

❧ Stickers (with horse-related designs) and tiny prize ribbons for page trims

❧ Spray polyurethane

INSIDE THE WINNER'S CIRCLE

·············◆·············

▲ Inside, each shaped page can nicely hold one vertical and one horizontal photograph; mount the photographs with photo-mount squares.

• Trim the pages with a scattering of stickers and little prize ribbons.

• If desired, add an inscription or journal entry (page 68) inside the front cover or to the album pages.

OUR
Kitty
CATS!

CELEBRATING FELINE CHARMS

C ats are so distinctive—those bright-blue Siamese eyes, that soft copper-colored coat. Try picking up some of their most characteristic colors and using them in the design of a scrapbook page. You'll be surprised how effective color can be in reflecting a cat's look and personality. You can also try hand-painting the paper cut-outs on pages 209–210 for another kind of personalized effect; they can even be used as frames for little bits of memorable information about your feline friends. Always shoot lots of pictures of your cats. As with children, try getting down to their level. And take some photos with their owners, too; there's nothing like a pet to prompt the warmest, most genuine smiles.

Ashley, who can be seen in some of the following pages, is my son Thomas's gold-haired domestic tiger cat.

YOU WILL NEED:

* Basic supplies (see page 42)

Supplies for this scrapbook:

* Spiral bound album with white cover and 10" x 10" pages
* Acid-free papers in assorted colors for page decorations
* Acid-free papers for paper-cut designs (see pages 209–210)
* Paints, colored pencils, or markers for detailing paper-cut designs (optional)
* Protective clear plastic sleeves

A PURR-FECT COVER

◄ Cut concentric squares, alternating a bright color (one you plan to repeat inside the album) with white, making the bottom colored layer 7 7/8 inches across, the next 5 3/16 inches across, then 4 1/4 inches, 3 1/2 inches, and 1 1/2 inches, ending with a 1-inch white square.

• Enlarge (page 50) the patterns for the cat and mouse corners on page 209. Following the directions for "How to Make Paper-Cut Designs," page 63, cut four cat corners and eight mouse corners as shown, underlining the cut-out area with the contrasting paper.

• Arrange the pieces in place and follow the photograph and "Making a Collage" on page 85, carefully aligning the corner set along the sides to form a diamond pattern as shown.

Color It Beautiful

Color is crucial to planning your album. Colors fall into either "warm" or "cool" categories, with the warmest being on the red-yellow-orange end of the spectrum, and the coolest being on the blue-green-purple side. Warmer colors, such as yellow, have the effect of advancing toward the viewer, while cooler colors, blue, for example, seems to recede.

Establishing a spectrum of colors produces a more harmonious feeling than you would get from an album devoted entirely to closely matched colors.

FRAMING THE CAT

························◆························

▶ These two pages use the paper-cut cat frame. The left one was made in a fresh green, in the vertical position the picture required, and the right in a warm royal blue. (The frame is designed to be used either way.)

• A border composed of the cat's name repeated all around finishes off the page.

Great Frames, Etc.

The cut-art frame patterns can be enlarged or slightly reduced (however, if used too small, they will be difficult to cut). This will enable you to use your frames with different-sized photographs. Parts of the frame pattern can be used separately. Yarn balls at the corners will make good corner mounts.

❝When I play with my cat, who knows if I am not a pastime to her more than she is to me?❞

—Montaigne

Cut paper illustrations by Andrea Wisnewski

MOLLY·MOLLY·MOLLY·MOLLY·MOLLY·MOLLY

CAT AND MOUSE

▼ You can decorate each page with individually made paper-cut designs. (See Our Best [Barking] Friend on page 174 for instructions on the use of paper-cut designs and how to work with color patterns.)

• The large photograph is mounted over orange and royal blue rectangles, cut with borders extending about ½ inch for each layer. Paper-cut mouse corners, blue over white, are added to the picture corners. Add glue just to the short outer edges of the corners to allow the photograph corners to slip in under the long edges.

CHING CHANG CHARMING

▼ The large paper-cut cat frame on page 209, cut from royal blue and placed over white, is positioned horizontally to fit the photograph. A matching blue strip underlines the white name tag that sports two paper-cut cat corners (page 209), blue over white.

THOMAS AND ASHLEY

▶ The photograph is mounted on a bright green backing and is topped with the delicately hand-painted paper-cut design (page 210) of a cat standing in matching green grass. If you are not a painter, simply cut the shape from white or green paper.

Great Details

Painters can put their skills to good use on these pages. Even the heart-shaped corners have painted details, as well as the heart-shaped larger designs. You can choose to paper-cut the motifs, leave them uncut and paint in the details, or use a combination, cutting some details and painting others. As you arrange the pieces on your page, swing the photograph to a diagonal position for a more dynamic collage.

OH ASHLEY!

▶ The underlying copper paper matches the copper tones of the cat's fur and is strikingly set off by the purple border.

• To make the heart trims, use the pattern for the paper-cut heart on page 210, but cut the cross strips no longer than the width of the heart. Slip the tip of the X-acto knife under the little bridge between the slits on the heart, and gently lift it up to make it easier to slide the cross strip through.

• Add decorative trim pieces to the top and bottom of the photograph as shown, clipping off the corner edges.

EXTENDING A PAW

▼ The copper and purple accents were used in the photograph mountings and for the paper-cut mouse corners. An X-acto knife was used to trim the unwanted background from the top picture, leaving just the cat's extended paw silhouetted. Notice how the extra-long photograph below was used to emphasize the length of the stretched-out cat.

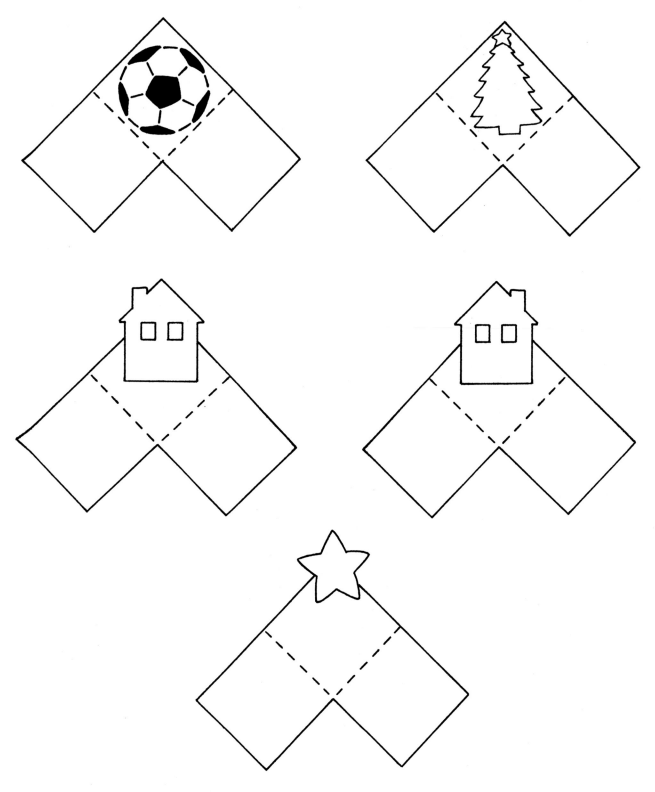

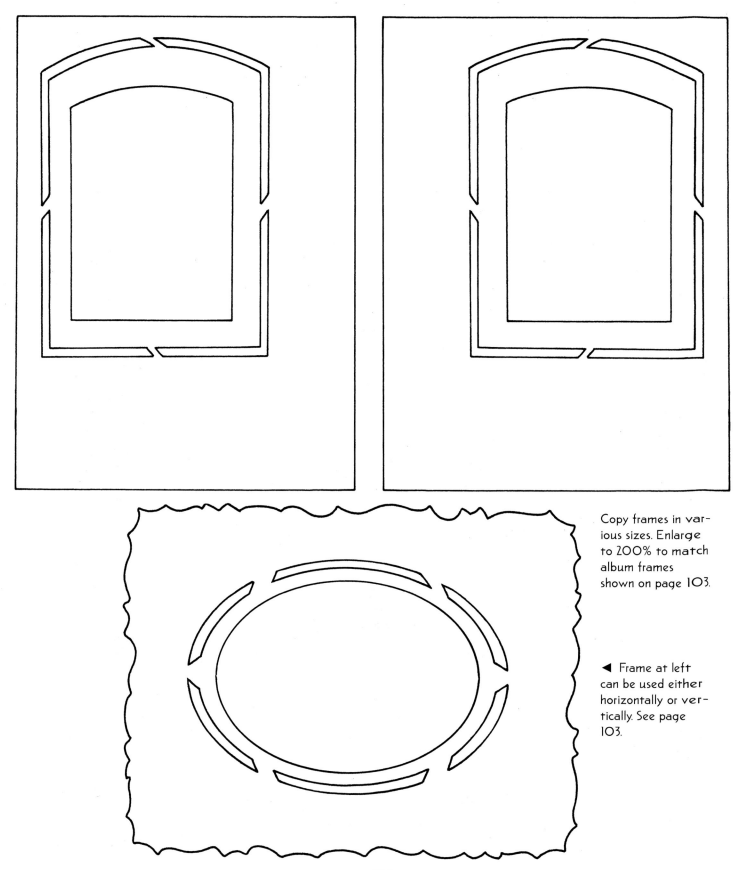

Copy frames in various sizes. Enlarge to 200% to match album frames shown on page 103.

◀ Frame at left can be used either horizontally or vertically. See page 103.

THE SOCCER BOOK TEMPLATE

▶ Soccer Ball pattern. Copy to desired size or enlarge to 150% to match size used in the album on page 128.

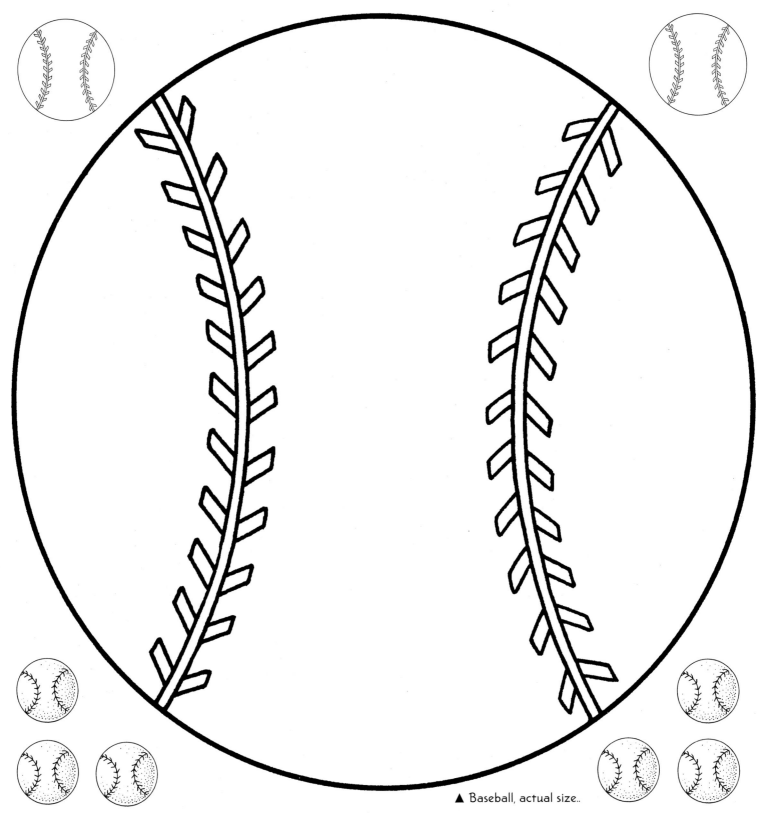

▲ Baseball, actual size..

BACK TO SCHOOL TEMPLATE

◆

▲▼ Actual size.

ZACHARY'S BAR MITZVAH TEMPLATES

◆

BOOKPLATES

These bookplates can be duplicated and inscribed to give your scrapbook a personal dedication when added to the inside of the front cover. Make them the desired size to fit your book.

A Scrapbook created by

For—

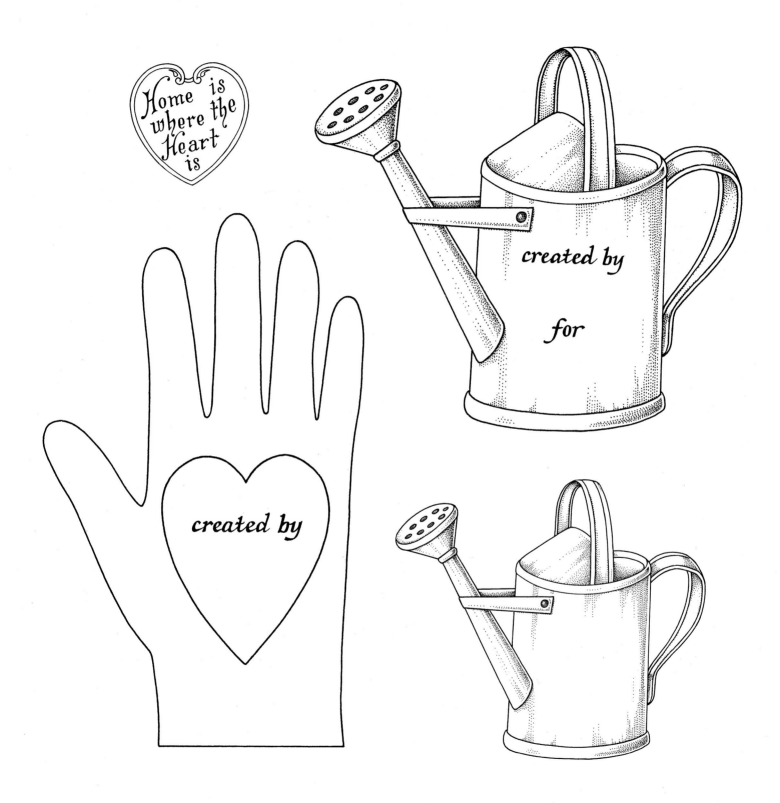

Home is where the Heart is

created by

for

created by